#FEESMUSTFALL
AND ITS AFTERMATH

With photographs of the photovoice project
"Violence and Wellbeing in the Student Movement"

#FEESMUSTFALL AND ITS AFTERMATH

VIOLENCE, WELLBEING AND THE STUDENT MOVEMENT IN SOUTH AFRICA

Thierry M. Luescher, Angelina Wilson Fadiji, Keamogetse G. Morwe

Antonio Erasmus, Tshireletso S. Letsoalo, Seipati B. Mokhema

FUNDING INFORMATION

Research for this work and its publication was co-funded by The National Research Foundation of South Africa, grant no. 118522 and The Andrew W. Mellon Foundation grant no. 1802-05403.

PROJECT INFORMATION

#FeesMustFall and its Aftermath: Violence, Wellbeing and the Student Movement in South Africa is an output of the overall research project "The New South African Student Movement: From #RhodesMustFall to #FeesMustFall" and particularly the sub-project "Violence and Wellbeing in the Context of the Student Movement". The project is led by Prof. Thierry M. Luescher. The sub-project is co-led by Prof. Thierry M. Luescher, Dr Keamogetse G. Morwe and Dr Angelina Wilson Fadiji.

Please cite as:

Luescher, T.M., Wilson Fadiji, A., Morwe, K.G., Erasmus, A., Letsoalo, T.S. & Mokhema, S.B. (2022). *#FeesMustFall and its Aftermath: Violence, Wellbeing and the Student Movement in South Africa*. HSRC Press.

Distributed in Africa by Blue Weaver

Tel: +27 (0) 21 701 4477

Email: info@blueweaver.co.za

www.blueweaver.co.za

Distributed in Europe and the United Kingdom by Eurospan Distribution Services (EDS)

Tel: +44 (0) 17 6760 4972

Fax: +44 (0) 17 6760 1640

www.eurospanbookstore.com

Distributed in the US, its possessions, Canada, and Asia by Lynne Rienner Publishers, Inc.

Tel: +1 303-444-6684

Fax: +1 303-444-0824

Email: cservice@rienner.com

www.rienner.com

Copyedited, designed, and typeset by Jive Media Africa, PO Box 22106, Mayors Walk, Pietermaritzburg, 3208, South Africa

www.jivemedia.co.za

Printed by Novus Print

CONTENTS

ACKNOWLEDGEMENTS

FeesMustFall and its Aftermath: Violence, Wellbeing and the Student Movement in South Africa comes from the research and archiving project "The New South African Student Movement: From #RhodesMustFall to #FeesMustFall" and especially its subproject "Violence and Wellbeing in the Context of the Student Movement". Its aim is to spark dialogue among all the parties – the minister and officials in the Department of Higher Education and Training and its entities, members of parliament and the relevant portfolio committees, the leadership of public universities, the leadership and members of the police service and private security services, student leaders and activists, and the public at large – on ways to curb violence during student protests and ensure policy and practices in the universities, colleges and beyond, support equitable access to quality learning, student engagement and success.

Credit for the idea to develop a research project on #FeesMustFall and the student movement of 2015/16 must go to Prof. Saleem Badat, then the Director of the International Higher Education and Strategic Projects programme at the Andrew W. Mellon Foundation in New York, who encouraged Prof. Thierry M. Luescher to develop a project proposal. The original proposal of June 2016, which included a Photovoice component, was drawn up by Prof. Thierry M. Luescher as principal investigator with support from Dr Leigh-Ann Naidoo and Prof. Shose Kessi, and additional input by Dr Omar Badsha, Mr Carl Collison, Prof. Lis Lange, Mr Nkululeko Makhubu, Mr Taabo Mugume, and Ms Khubu Zulu. The proposal to conduct specifically an investigation into violence and wellbeing in the context of the student movement was drawn up by Prof. Thierry M. Luescher as principal investigator, Dr Keamogetse G. Morwe as co-principal investigator and Dr Angelina Wilson Fadiji as project manager.

THIS PROJECT AND THE BOOK WOULD NOT HAVE BEEN POSSIBLE WITHOUT THE FUNDING FROM:

- The National Research Foundation of South Africa, grant no. 118522
- The Andrew W. Mellon Foundation, grant no. 1802-05403
- The Human Sciences Research Council of South Africa

The main authors of this book would also like to acknowledge the following persons who contributed significantly to the success of the project:

- Ms Tania Fraser, the project's administrator, who ensured that the project expenditures are within the defined parameters, despite the research team's grand ideas.
- Mr Carl Collison, who curated the 105 pictures generated by the Photovoice process into the exhibition "Aftermath", which is presently hosted by South African History Online and is travelling university campuses in South Africa and abroad under the stewardship of Mr Aldo Brincat, our travel exhibition chaperone.
- Mr Nkululeko Makhubo and Ms Kulani Mlambo, our Masters interns who helped identify student activists and participated in some of the Photovoice workshops.

Last but not least, we would like to acknowledge all the student participants of Photovoice workshops whose reflections this book presents:

- University of the Western Cape: Azania Simthandile Tyhali, Sphelele Khumalo, Ncedisa Bemnyama, Asandiswa Bomvana, and Siyasanga Ndwayi.
- University of Venda: Bob Sandile Masango, Abednego Sam Mandhlazi, Blessing Mavhuru, Frans Sello Mokwele, Hlulani C. Chabalala, Tshepo Raseala, Anyway Mikioni, Mulaedza Mashapha, Dimakatso Ngobeni, and a student who wants to remain anonymous.
- University of the Free State: Tshepang Mahlatsi, Tshiamo Malatji, Thabo Mpho Miya, Sonwabile Dwaba, Kamohelo Maphike, Xola Zatu, and two students who want to remain anonymous.
- University of Fort Hare: Madoda Ludidi, Yolokazi Mfuto, Litha Dyomfana, Siphelele Mancobeni, Wandisile Sixoto, and Akhona Manyenyeza.
- Durban University of Technology: Khulekani Ngcobo, Robert Thema, Lesley Ngazire, Siphephelo (Shange) Mthembu, Nomfundo Zakwe, and Thalente Hadebe.

We also thank the academics and student affairs practitioners who participated at the World Café discussions at the University of the Western Cape, University of Venda, and University of Fort Hare.

Finally, we thank our publishers, the team at Jive Media and the HSRC Press, and the anonymous peer reviewers of the manuscript for their advice and support to realise this project and enhance the quality and scholarly value of the book.

FOREWORD

TRANSFORMATION AND THE STUDENT MOVEMENT: THEN, NOW, AND IN FUTURE - BY SALEEM BADAT

Observing the South African student protests from my then location at The Andrew W. Mellon Foundation in New York, I successfully motivated in 2015 a grant to the Human Sciences Research Council for research and writing on the protests. Based on my past work on black higher education student politics under apartheid and my intimate decades-long involvement in higher education, my interest was in research that deciphered the meanings and explained the student protests of 2015-16, including the continuities and discontinuities with past protests and especially what was distinctive about the contemporary protests. I noted that in 2015-16, there was a re-entry in very visible ways of South African university students onto the higher education terrain. This was not to say that students were not part of steering and shaping higher education through institutional governance structures or that there were no student protests between 1994 and 2015. There were, especially at the historically black universities and at those institutions that were merged as part of the restructuring of the higher education landscape after 2000.

However, it was being suggested that there was something especially dramatic and distinctive about the 2015-16 protests, and I was curious wherein lay the drama and distinctiveness of the protests. Did they have to do with the breadth and depth of mobilisation, the targets of opposition and the nature of the demands? Or was it that they possibly served as a salutary reminder of the tardy pace and limited degree of transformation in higher education? And, given the connections between higher education and society, did they signal also impatience with change and the limits of change in the wider economic, political, and social domains? How should the 2015-16 protests be theorised and their character and significance for universities, higher education, and the wider polity and society be understood? Were the 2015-16 protests, I wondered, one manifestation of the "organic crisis" of South African higher education, a crisis that necessitated urgent and major "formative action" on the part of the state and other key actors? The reality was that state funding was grossly inadequate to support universities to undertake their critical purposes – produce knowledge, cultivate high quality graduates, engage meaningfully with diverse communities – to ensure that learning and teaching, research, and institutional culture were transformed and to help to realise environmentally sustainable economic development, equity, social justice, and the extension and deepening of democracy.

I argued for imaginative theorisation, extensive description, and rigorous analysis of the 2015-16 student protests and the need for fully documenting the trajectory, dynamics, character, and significance of the student protest movement that emerged and grew during the course of 2015 and continued during 2016. Scholarship had to avoid both spectacular claims about their meaning, as well as fanciful predictions about their future trajectory and significance; it had to illuminate and convey understanding of the protests in all their richness and complexity. Given my location in 2015-16, I could only explicate key concepts and pose questions that I hoped that, when supplemented with additional concepts and questions, could provide a generative and robust framework for analysing the student protests. My concern was with appropriate questions about the protests, rather than immediate answers about their trajectory, dynamics, character, and significance.

A collaborative endeavour between researchers at the Human Sciences Research Council and the University of Venda and former student activists and student leaders, *#FeesMustFall and its Aftermath: Violence, Wellbeing and the Student Movement in South Africa* is a welcome contribution to efforts to document and understand the 2015-16 national student protests associated with #RhodesMustFall, #FeesMustFall, #EndOutsourcing, and other movements. While the research and writing undertaken to date extends beyond this book, *#FeesMustFall and its Aftermath* makes recourse to Photovoice as a research method to document aspects of the student protests. The book contains over 100 photographs, captions, and narratives that arise from action research conducted with student leaders and activists on five university campuses that were involved in the 2015 and 2016 student protests, the universities of the Western Cape, Free State, Venda and Fort Hare, and the Durban University of Technology. These universities were selected deliberately to highlight the experiences of students at universities that, unlike the universities of Cape Town and Witwatersrand, were not in the public limelight in 2015 and 2016 but whose experiences could be more representative of the sector as a whole.

At the Photovoice workshops that were conducted, the students were encouraged to submit photographs that, in their view, best reflected their experiences of the violence that led to and occurred during the student protests, and photographs that represented wellbeing resources that helped them to manage and perhaps overcome their experiences of violence. During the workshops, beginning in mid-2019 and continuing well into the first COVID-19 pandemic lockdown in 2020, the students presented and discussed each of their photos, captioned them, and provided brief narratives to contextualise the photos and reflect on what they meant to them. The students' work featured as small exhibitions on their university campuses for staff members and especially for Student Affairs practitioners and academics.

During 2021, the research team and some of the student participants classified many of the photographs, captions, and narratives from the five universities into various themes. These themes include the context and reasons for protesting; students' mobilisation for protest; protest itself;

the state's response to protests; state violence; student wellbeing; and the wellbeing resources drawn upon by students. As part of curating the book, the research team conceptualised and elaborated these themes in more detail. In presenting the research to the scholarly community, policy makers, and the public at large in the form of a photobook, the goal is to raise awareness about the unacceptably high levels of violence on university campuses and its impact on student wellbeing. In engaging university leaders and policy makers, who at times may be either unresponsive or tardy in their responses to student claims and grievances, students sometimes commit violence directed at other students, staff, facilities, and buildings, or are themselves subject directly to violence at the hands of private security companies and state security forces, or become observers of violence.

This book focuses exclusively on the reflections of 35 former student activists and student leaders from five universities, without seeking to "balance" them with views of university leaders and managers, academics, other staff, and security personnel who were involved in the on- and off-campus contestations and conflict, providing an unadulterated and unique insight into their perspectives. To present the perspectives is not necessarily to agree with the perspectives. It is, however, an invitation to ponder on the perspectives, to engage with them and to agree or disagree to differing degrees. Above all, it is an invitation to draw lessons on how our universities, society, and the state can become more affirming institutions, support more fully the 1997 White Paper's goals of equity of access, opportunity, and success, and to continue to more

intentionally, purposefully, creatively, and consistently decolonise and transform our universities and higher education.

Various chapters frame and intersperse the thematic photo narrative chapters. Among other things, these chapters conceptually and methodologically frame the research and writing, address issues of student struggle, space, and gender, discuss the authors procedural and advocacy goals and reflections on the knowledge and associated contributions of the book. Across the book are powerful, graphic, and "iconic" photographs – the 2015 and 2016 student protests in snapshots.

Elsewhere I have observed that, instead of holding great promise and being an ennobling adventure for students, higher education was in danger of becoming a killing field of ambitions, aspirations, and dreams, in a context where those who graduate from universities enjoy the prospects of more decent jobs, greater earnings, and higher standards of living than those without university qualifications. The authors likewise note about black, and especially working class and rural, poor students that "they often come to university not only carrying their own hopes and aspirations for a prosperous future, but also bearing the expectation of generations." Given this, "to then find themselves in contexts, where so many odds seem to be stacked against them academically and economically, and too frequently also culturally, socially, and politically, and therefore where dreams and aspirations seem to evaporate within quarters and semesters, the choices are limited: struggle or resign" (p. 1). To fail as universities, state, and society to ensure meaningful physical and epistemological access, opportunity, and success for students is to inflict different kinds of violence on students. Given economic, social, and political conditions and the stakes, that there was violence of various kinds is not surprising. The authors comment that "students become witnesses, victims, and perpetrators of violence" (p. 3). However, their research was not "interested in violence per se or in establishing who fired the first rubber bullet or threw the first stone; [they] "rather wanted to explore the ways that students understand violence, recover from exposure to violence, and restore some form of wellbeing" (p. 3).

Violence and wellbeing are juxtaposed from the outset in the title of the book and in various places in the text. The juxtaposition is powerful and appropriate. The authors openly declare that they are not disinterested spectators. Nor should they necessarily be. It is not possible to undertake value-free social science research; everyone proceeds from a social standpoint, thinks and acts from a certain location in the social hierarchy. The supposed irrelevance of "the persona of the scholar," and the idea that scholars function as "value-neutral analysts" is a key feature of Eurocentric epistemology (Wallerstein, 1997, p. 95). Yet "it is necessary to focus on the knower," because the "knower is always implicated, geo- and body-politically in the known," despite the fact that "modern epistemology managed to conceal both and built the figure of the detached observer, a neutral seeker of truth and objectivity" (Mignolo, 2011, p. 119, p. 123). Grosfoguel notes that "we always speak from a particular location in the power structures. Nobody escapes the class, sexual,

gender, spiritual, linguistic, geographical, and racial hierarchies" within which we are located (2007, p. 213). Similarly, Haraway persuasively argues that knowledge-making is about "location" and "situated and embodied knowledges", not about "transcendence and splitting of subject and object" – scholars have to be "answerable for what we learn how to see" (1988, p. 583). The flaw of "Western epistemic traditions…that claim detachment of the known from the knower" is that "they rest on a division between mind and world, or between reason and nature as an ontological *a priori*" (Mbembe, 2016, p. 32). In this approach, "the knowing subject is enclosed in itself and peeks out at a world of objects and produces supposedly objective knowledge of those objects. The knowing subject is thus able to know the world without being part of that world and he or she is by all accounts able to produce knowledge that is supposed to be universal and independent of context" (Mbembe, 2016, p. 33).

These observations are simultaneously a rejoinder to criticism and dismissal of activist research as being biased, flawed, lacking rigour, and not to be taken seriously. There are challenges but no contradiction between being socially committed and undertaking dispassionate, rigorous, and high quality scholarly research. It is what engaged activist research is about. Activist research "must be judged on its own merits – the design and logic of the project, the quality of the evidentiary base, the analytical power of the argument, ways in which the scholarship resolves anomalies and opens up new areas of inquiry, while challenging the inherited orthodoxies" (Isaacman, 2003, p. 8).

The authors' concern, admirably, "as students and researchers of higher education is student wellbeing" (p. 21). And rightly it is "especially, the wellbeing, flourishing and success of the most vulnerable students in higher education: those who struggle to succeed in a context of the interlocking matrix of oppression that characterises the intersections of various markers of social identity at university: class, disability, gender, language and ethnicity, parental level of education, prior schooling, race, sexual orientation, and so forth" (p. 3). To their credit, the authors recognise that the "timely and legitimate" student demands "which can be summarised as free, decolonised, quality higher education" (p. 2) require advocacy not just within higher education and universities but also depend ultimately on a "new kind of society, politics, and leadership" (p.4). Their hope is "to contribute to flourishing: flourishing students and young people; a flourishing society; and a flourishing Africa" (p. 21). "Undertaking advocacy work [was] always…one of the purposes" (p. 107) of the author's research. They understand advocacy as "telling the truth, however inconvenient" and action that at multiple levels purposefully defends, represents, and advances social justice for socially disadvantaged and marginalised individuals and social groups (p. 107).

Fast forward to 2022, a substantial improvement in opportunity and outcomes for black, and especially rural, poor, and working class students remains elusive. If "race" previously shaped access, opportunity, and success, social class now largely conditions these. These realities undermine the significant expansion in enrolments that have occurred post-1994 and suggest, as the higher

education ministry itself acknowledges, that higher education "is unable to effectively support and provide reasonable opportunities for success to its students" and that there is "inefficient use of the country's resources" (Department of Higher Education and Training, 2013, p. 2). They also compromise equity, social inclusion, and development. Macroeconomic policies and the state in various ways put significant brakes on radical change in higher education. Racial capitalism, patriarchy, and the embracement of neo-liberal orthodoxies result in a highly truncated "non-racial and non-sexist system of higher education", which constitutes severe impediments to "equity of access and fair chances of success" for subaltern social classes and constrains "eradicating all forms of unfair discrimination" and "advancing redress for past inequalities" (Department of Education, 1997, p. 114). The state has failed to address difficult dilemmas: its attempt to balance equity, quality, and development imperatives has produced largely historical rectification for individuals rather than fundamental institutional structural transformation.

To fail as universities, state, and society to ensure meaningful physical and epistemological access, opportunity, and success for students is to inflict different kinds of violence on students.

Given the book's title *#FeesMustFall and its Aftermath*, it would have been interesting to hear how the student activists and student leaders view the current university terrain. Do current conditions in higher education demonstrate some of the limits of the 2015 and 2016 student political action? While students are a critical force and catalyst of reforms and transformation, might deep reflection and change be required in the nature and content of student political activism? Could there be doubts today about the transformative potential of focusing largely on personal pain, trauma, and identity in ways that are unconnected with the question of political power and the material conditions required for social justice (Kelly, 2016)? Student organisations created a new higher education terrain and agenda, but since then have exemplified little creative, consistent, and concerted national and institutional-level engagement with that agenda. Institutional transformation and the strategies and tactics of change and its resourcing have seemingly been ceded to university administrations, the state, and committed academics. Might new generations of student leaders need to build effective alliances among student formations and between them and other non-student class, popular, and professional organisations and movements? Without achieving a confluence with other social forces, are student movements not in danger of being characterised by "brief brush fires and relapses into passivity by the majority" (Hobsbawm, 1973, p. 265)? Of course, the challenges to building strong and durable student organisation and maintaining effective mobilisation and engagement are considerable.

One academic peer-reviewer describes the book as a work of "exceptionally high standard" that is "strikingly original and beautifully presented", has "an intellectually rich and compassionate conceptual approach" and that advances a methodology that "will continue to produce applied social-work and counselling insights on student wellbeing". Thierry Luescher, Keamogetse Morwe, Angelina Wilson Fadiji, Tshireletso Letsoalo, Seipati Mokhema, and Antonio Erasmus must be commended for persevering with and publishing this rich and innovative book.

Saleem Badat
Research Professor
Humanities Institute, University of KwaZulu-Natal

CHAPTER 1
STUDENT WELLBEING, TO US

We hope to contribute to flourishing:
flourishing students and young people, a flourishing society, and a
flourishing Africa.

TOWARDS FLOURISHING

To bridge the gap between rich and poor, white and black, male and female, historically advantaged and disadvantaged; to be able to climb the social and economic ladder, have social mobility and realise economic emancipation, education in general, and higher education more especially, provide a determining mechanism (Soudien, 2021). Yet, despite huge efforts, the stakes remain enormously, often unbearably high for black students from socio-economically disadvantaged backgrounds to access, progress through, and succeed in South Africa's universities. They often come to university not only carrying their own hopes and aspirations for a prosperous future, but also bearing the expectation of generations (Swartz et al., 2018). Then to find themselves in contexts where so many odds seem to be stacked against them academically and economically, and too frequently also culturally, socially, and politically, and where therefore dreams and aspirations seem to evaporate within quarters and semesters, the choice is limited: struggle or resign.

Mlungisi Cele showed in his remarkable study of student activism at the University of the Western Cape (UWC) that students' struggles take on different types of action. He distinguishes between individual, survivalist strategies and collective action; and between actions that conform to expected norms and others he termed non-normative (Cele, 2015; Cele et al., 2016). In 2015/16, a nationwide wave of collective, non-normative student action – or, more concretely, a massive wave of student protests – washed across the South African higher education landscape, leaving it forever changed. The demands of the students, which can be summarised as free, decolonised, quality higher education, were widely acknowledged as timely and legitimate, even if the students' ways of raising them were not always endorsed (Habib, 2019).

The 2015/16 student movement, known by campaign hashtags such as #RhodesMustFall, #BlackStudentMovement, #OpenStellenbosch, #FeesMustFall, #EndOutsourcing, #NationalShutdown, #RUReferenceList, and so forth, has been studied from a variety of disciplinary perspectives, including historical, political, and educational viewpoints, and for different purposes. Books and journals have been filled with the writings of student activists (e.g., Chikane, 2018; Langa, 2017; Ngcaweni & Ngacaweni, 2018; Luescher et al., 2020), the reflections of vice-chancellors (Jansen, 2017; Habib, 2018), and the research of higher education specialists and academics (Booysen, 2016; Nyamnjoh, 2016). Theses have been examined and degrees conferred (e.g., Ahmed, 2019; Mandyoli, 2019; Naidoo, 2020; Ntuli, 2020). Policies have been changed and new discourses and higher education practices have emerged (Jansen, 2019) during and in the aftermath of #FeesMustFall. However, little has been said about the biographical impact of the activist movement on the student activists' lives. Few publications in South Africa

have started to consider this, and the book commissioned by the Council on Higher Education, *Reflections of South African Student Leaders, 1994–2017*, is an exception (Luescher et al., 2020). Some former #FeesMustFall activists continue to make the news, having become members of parliament, like Nompendulo Mkhatshwa and Vuyani Pambo, who were student leaders at the University of the Witwatersrand (Wits) in 2015/16, and Naledi Chirwa of the University of Pretoria (UP). Other student leaders, like Kanya Cekeshe of the Cape Peninsula University of Technology and Bonginkosi Khanyile of the Durban University of Technology (DUT), served jail time for their actions during #FeesMustFall.

> 66
>
> *Our concern as students and researchers of higher education is student wellbeing, especially the wellbeing, flourishing, and success of the most vulnerable students in higher education…*
>
> 99

The first wave of #RhodesMustFall-related and #FeesMustFall-related protests in 2015 is frequently considered as quite peaceful. Certainly, there were many moments of frustration, aggression, and confrontation, but violence on the sides of the state, the institutions, and the students tended to be within bounds. Unlike the campus culture on many historically black and rural university campuses and universities of technology, where violent protesting has become shockingly normalised over the years (Luescher et al., 2020), the protests at the University of Cape Town (UCT), the University of the Free State (UFS), and Wits, to mention but a few, under the banners of #RhodesMustFall, #SteynMustFall, and #FeesMustFall during 2015, involved little violence. There were certainly isolated events where students and police or private security clashed painfully. However, the situation turned rapidly in the final part of, and after, the October 2015 #FeesMustFall campaign. For instance, the #FeesWillFall protests at UWC turned violent in late October and continued into November 2015. In February 2016, violence broke out at UCT, in part during the #Shackville demonstration, but also as part of other campaigns. At UFS, a peaceful picket to end the exploitative practice of outsourcing the most vulnerable workers was assaulted into submission first on the #ShimlaPark rugby field, and then for a week on the campus, with police invading student spaces, brutalising and radicalising the student movement there. From Rhodes University (RU) in the Eastern Cape and their campaign to end "rape culture", to DUT in KwaZulu-Natal, student protests at institution after institution turned violent. Since 2015, #FeesMustFall has experienced several reruns. In each case, students become witnesses, victims, and perpetrators of violence.

The research project that gave rise to this book was never interested in violence per se or in establishing who fired the first rubber bullet or threw the first stone. We rather wanted to explore the ways that students understand violence, recover from exposure to violence, and restore some form of wellbeing. On the one hand, the study of violence is often limited to the pathology associated with it, and little consideration is given to the strengths and resources drawn on in the wake of the experiences of violence. On the other hand, wellbeing research often focuses specifically on the positives of life to the neglect of "the dance of the positives and negatives" that so often produces real flourishing in individuals (Wilson Fadiji et al., forthcoming). It was with this in mind that a Photovoice study was designed, and it is against this that this book aims to contribute – conceptually, practically, and politically – to positive change by presenting students' experiences of violence and aggression during the 2015/16 student movement, as well as the resources drawn upon by students to restore their wellbeing and flourish amidst such experiences.

Our concern as students and researchers of higher education is student wellbeing, especially the wellbeing, flourishing, and success of the most vulnerable students in higher education: those who struggle to succeed in a context of the interlocking matrix of oppression (Collins, 2019) that characterises the intersections of various markers of social identity at university: class, disability, gender, language and ethnicity, parental level of education, prior schooling, race, sexual orientation, and so forth.

Wellbeing as defined in positive psychology is a precondition for learning (Yu et al., 2018), and the correlation between wellbeing and academic achievement is significant (Bücker et al., 2018). Especially in the aftermath of #FeesMustFall, universities have seen rising incidences of mental health problems and suicides among students (Schreiber, 2018). Our concern is not to apportion blame or responsibility. Our concern is to contribute to a higher education system and to institutions that are non-violent, a society that is non-violent. We hope to contribute to university environments that are fit to develop critically constructive, active citizens; graduates that have the skills, knowledge, and attitudes to make a successful transition into the world of work; well-rounded young people who find their place in our shared humanity and as stewards of this planet and the life it is a home to. We hope to advocate – through the process of research, through knowledge and advocacy work – a new kind of society, politics, and leadership. We hope to contribute to flourishing: flourishing students and young people, a flourishing society, and a flourishing Africa.

To state our understanding of some concepts upfront, we want to share five quotes respectively dealing with violence, decolonisation, #FeesMustFall, wellbeing and leadership.

ON VIOLENCE

"What is violence? The nature of violence may be more complex than the seeming simplicity of this question, not least because violence can take many forms (e.g., spectacle, symbolic, embodied, systemic, implicit in the everyday conditions of life) and can be mobilised to bring attention to socio-political and economic challenges.

How a person understands violence is influenced by whether the individual has lived with or had bodily encounter(s) with violence that disrupt the experience of personhood and other aspects of human life. Or, one may encounter violence as an object of study using the "logic of things". Here, the physical body, both as a site of violence and because of its tangibility, offers an easy site for the study of violence, even though the physical body is by no means the only dimension touched by violence.

Understanding violence is also complicated by two other issues. On the one hand, violence is a dynamic phenomenon capable of shifting its meanings, effects, and agents across time and space, such that a given person, for instance, can be a witness, victim, and perpetrator of violence. On the other hand, democratic South Africa has to contend with a threefold tension. First, the demand for democracy was a response to the violence and inhumanity of apartheid and the regimes from which apartheid was derived. Second, the sociopolitical birthing of democracy went through a long gestation period (over 350 years at least) between state and insurgent violence. Third, there was the perception that the dawn of democracy signalled a break with violence – difficulties and conflicts, in a democracy, would be resolved without resorting to violence. And yet, some democratic governments, including that of South Africa, deploy violence against their citizens in the name of protecting national interests, and ordinary people continue to use violence" (Khanyile, 2020).

ON DECOLONISATION

"Spivak (1994) defines 'epistemic violence' as the Eurocentric and Western domination and subjugation of the [former] colonial subjects and the misconception of their understanding and perception of the world. This is a result of 'violence of imperialistic epistemic, social and disciplinary inscription' (1994, p. 80)… Epistemic violence persists in post-apartheid South Africa, where the higher education system, rooted in colonial and apartheid exploitation and racism, has obliterated nearly all the linkages that black students may have with the prescribed texts, propagated narratives, debates and learning on the one side, and their history, lived experiences and dreams on the other side."

Decolonisation of higher education is "about justice that addresses the epistemic violence of colonial knowledge and colonial thought" (Pillay, 2015). South Africa needs a higher education system to develop graduates and intellectuals who can address the epistemic violence of the past and present and who will go on to rewrite the "histories and humanity [of both South Africa and Africa] so cruelly seized and denied by Europe" (Zeleza, 2009, p. 116) throughout centuries.

Decolonisation requires a large mass of people demanding change on the campuses and in society. They will have to confront the "official orthodoxy" (Mudimbe, 1985, p. 209) and "consciously disrupt the status quo" (Nwadeyi, 2016). Social and structural change seldom happens anywhere in the world without activism, advocacy, dissent, disruption and protest. The powerful and influential don't simply give in because it is the right thing to do; they act only when they are compelled to do so by social movements and masses" (Heleta, 2016).

To bridge the gap between rich and poor, white and black, male and female, historically advantaged and disadvantaged; to be able to climb the social and economic ladder, have social mobility and realise economic emancipation, education in general, and higher education more especially, provide a determining mechanism.

ON #FEESMUSTFALL

"University students not only made the connections between the ways colonialism and apartheid have reproduced racial and class inequalities in South Africa, laid bare the ANC's broken promises and exposed the negative effects of neoliberalism, but also magnified class differences and the failures of university administrations and curriculums to transform racially. Ironically, of course, it took a rise in political organising on formerly white universities to push these issues into the public domain – for years, activists on mainly black campuses had been raising similar complaints. Still, the students were able to make vital connections to outsourcing on campuses and, crucially, began to agitate for free public higher education.

In what has since taken on mythical proportions, university students disrupted campuses, invented new vocabularies ("decolonisation", for example) and opened debates about the nature, extent and compromises which characterised the political transition from apartheid. In the process, they became the most significant national social movement since the end of apartheid – and also the first middle-class black grouping to challenge the government and white business openly on a grand scale. By the end of 2015, the country's president, Jacob Zuma, had caved in when he announced (at least temporarily) no future fee increases. The movement has since stalled due to a mix of political factors and reflects the general stasis in South African politics, but its impact is still felt widely" (Jacobs, 2015).

On the one hand, the study of violence is often limited to the pathology associated with it, and little consideration is given to the strengths and resources drawn on in the wake of the experiences of violence. On the other hand, wellbeing research often focuses specifically on the positives of life to the neglect of "the dance of the positives and negatives" that so often produces real flourishing in individuals.

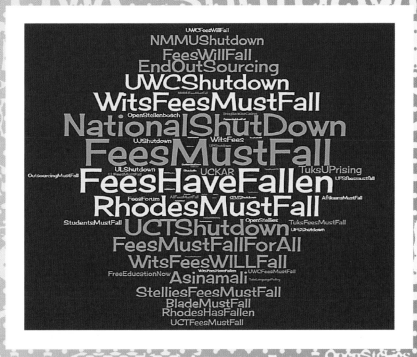

ON WELLBEING

"Flourishing does not mean being a 'well-defended fortress, invulnerable to the vicissitudes of life', but appreciating and even embracing the complex and ambivalent nature of life… Hence, the second wave of positive psychology is 'above all epitomised by a recognition of the fundamentally dialectical nature of wellbeing'.

The notion of dialectics points to 'this tension [which] describes the way in which binary opposites – such as positive and negative, or light and dark – while being diametrically opposed, are yet intimately connected and dependent upon each other for their very existence" (Lomas & Ivtzan, 2016).

ON LEADERWSHIP

"Great leaders will tell you that courage does not roar like a lion. Leaders who are coming together understand that most of the challenges we face, which are poverty and inequality, were not necessarily our fault; they were inherited from the past… We don't have to strangle each other. We just have to sit around the table and look at where we go from now. […] What we need: we need grown-ups. We need political leaders to be grown-ups and lead the way in terms of what kind of society we are building, because the kind of anger that we are peddling is gonna come back to bite us, all of us" (Madonsela, 2021).

CHAPTER 2

VIOLENCE, WELLBEING, AND A PHOTOBOOK

"

In thinking about the concept and layout of a scholarly book that can present the pictures and narratives from the research, we deliberately chose the somewhat contradictory format of a beautiful coffee table book and filled it with the shocking images of disillusionment, struggle, pain, fear, warlike mobilisation, and brutality, but also with promise, hope, resourcefulness, purpose, and a positive outlook towards the future of South Africa.

"

In a somewhat contradictory format, the book *#FeesMustFall and its Aftermath* details the reflections of 35 student activists from five South African universities of their experience of violence and wellbeing in relation to their involvement in the student movement. The student activists' narrations were facilitated by five researchers, a visual graphics editor, and a number of additional staff members over a project period of several years. Like the research process overall, this book is a truly collaborative achievement, designed to serve as a powerful tool to advocate awareness and change in the universities, the higher education policy sector, and the broader public.

Themed *#FeesMustFall and its Aftermath*, the book illustrates pictorially and with their narratives the former student activists' experiences of violence and wellbeing, as recalled in the aftermath of the 2015/16 student movement. The book also documents the journey of the research team in uncovering these student experiences and perspectives, in working with select groups of student activists from five different universities.

In thinking about the concept and layout of a scholarly book that can present the pictures and narratives from the research, we deliberately chose the somewhat contradictory

format of a beautiful coffee table book and filled it with the shocking images of disillusionment, struggle, pain, fear, warlike mobilisation, and brutality, but also with promise, hope, resourcefulness, purpose, and a positive outlook towards the future of South Africa. Contrary to the typical public relations "coffee table book", this book is not about beautifying reality. Many pictures are deliberately blurry, pixilated, or distorted. The text is deliberately not a brand manager's copy edit. Rather, the captions and short narratives that accompany the pictures are written by students in their own words and have been left to reflect their way of articulating their thoughts. As much as the book is written in a scholarly manner, it is meant to remain accessible to both academics and non-academics alike: an authentic witness for awareness raising, meaning-making, and informing educational decision makers, policy role players, stakeholders, and the general public, using the honest and provocative data and findings of the "Violence and Wellbeing" project's Photovoice work. By means of this choice of format, design, and layout, as well as authentic presentation and minimal analysis, we hope the students' narratives will be simultaneously more accessible and more impactful than using other scholarly means. Our approach to representation can be summarised in two sayings: "A picture is worth 1 000 words," and "Only the wearer of the shoe knows where it pinches".

As an output of an action research project with explicit political and advocacy goals (as well as scholarly and knowledge production goals), the book does not try to present a "balanced" account. This is a work whose trustworthiness is measured by the authenticity of the narratives it presents. It is a book that puts forth deliberatively the perspective of student activists. In that, it does not pretend to be more unbiased than some of the other books that were written in the aftermath of #FeesMustFall (e.g., by former vice-chancellors and others with vested interests in presenting themselves in a certain light).

Moreover, *#FeesMustFall and its Aftermath* – right from the conception of the research project to the point of publication of this book – has been an experimental project. Not in terms of our having a lack of conviction about its utility, but in our pursuit of it as a deliberate attempt to ensure that such sensitive and important subjects as violence on university campuses and student mental health and wellbeing are explored in a scholarly and methodical manner that will allow an authentic representation of students' experiences. To tackle questions of novelty of approach and findings that might emerge from scholars and practitioners in the field, we were intentional about ensuring methodological rigour (as documented in Luescher et al., 2021b), the empowerment of both students and practitioners alike, and accessibility of research findings to a wide audience. Still on novelty, the Photovoice methodology (to be explained in more detail in chapters 9 and 13), which has been used in similar studies on student experiences in South African universities (e.g., Cornell et al., 2016; Kessi & Cornell, 2015), was further enhanced by our adding to it a World Café methodology (Cooperrider & Whitney, 1999). During the World Café, university staff members – including academics, Student Affairs practitioners, and university managers – were invited to join in the final round of Photovoice sessions by being part of a collective process of reflecting on the exhibitions that students from their campus had curated in preceding days, while proffering possible solutions to the issue of violence and the quest for wellbeing.

REFLECTIONS ON VIOLENCE

The use of the term "violence" was critiqued in a review of a manuscript we submitted to one of the top scholarly journals in higher education studies. Our reviewers were of the opinion that the term was too evocative and should be toned down. We, however, retained the term because not only does it capture the physical altercations between students on campus and police or security services, but it was a term consistently used by students themselves to describe the way they understood their living and learning experiences on campus (as "institutional violence" and "epistemic violence"), their experience of South African society (as "structural violence") and their experiences during the student movement (as "physical violence").

These different uses of the term "violence" point to its varied manifestations in students' everyday lives. For instance, structural violence refers to the social structuring of society, where certain categories of persons and communities are practically permanently condemned to eke out a living at the margins, as subordinates, as have-nots (Khanyile, 2020). Degenaar (1990, p. 71) differentiates between physical violence and violation, where the former refers to the use of force against another resulting in injury, while the latter relates to a moral desecration and the disruption of an individual's integrity or dignity. It is possible for physical violence and violation to intersect, when bodily injuries also affect an individual's sense of dignity, humanity, and identity. The definitions highlighted here represent different ways in which "technical" language can be quite precise. For the young people in our study who describe their experiences of individual and collective injury and pain, distinguishing between the abstract and the concrete; the physical, emotional, psychological, and spiritual; the result of momentary action and a history of centuries of colonialism and apartheid, is trite – indeed, it is offensive.

The most important point is that violence of whatever nature should never be at the centre of students' experiences. However lived and understood, violence represents an unwanted experience that needs to be addressed and neutralised. Taking a wellbeing perspective in studying violence is no way to soothe the pain or make restitution; rather, it just highlights one aspect of the dire need for multipronged intervention in the higher education space. These assertions are only nuanced to some extent by our recognition that wellbeing involves a "dance of the positives and negatives of life" (Wilson Fadiji et al., forthcoming).

As an output of an action research project with explicit political and advocacy goals (as well as scholarly and knowledge production goals), the book does not try to present a "balanced" account. This is a work whose trustworthiness is measured by the authenticity of the narratives it presents.

THE GENESIS OF THE PROJECT

The inception of this project can be traced back to a hurried Skype call from New York in October 2015. Dr Saleem Badat, then the Program Director for International Higher Education and Strategic Projects at The Andrew W. Mellon Foundation called Dr Thierry Luescher to inquire about developments related to the student protests and urged him to "keep a finger on what is happening in the student movement with #FeesMustFall." Dr Badat indicated that Mellon would be willing to consider a creative project proposal on the protests and their implications for universities. In the course of elaborating that proposal and assembling a project consortium, Dr Shose Kessi from UCT first proposed Photovoice as a possible methodology. The Mellon-funded project ended up using, initially, in-depth interviewing as a method to engage former student activists and ordinary students. It took another two years and additional funding from the National Research Foundation to realise the idea of adopting Photovoice as a close-up, emancipatory method for working with former student leaders and activists of the 2015/16 era.

Indeed, it was in the collaboration between Dr Angelina Wilson Fadiji, psychologist and wellbeing specialist, then at the Human Sciences Research Council (HSRC); Dr Keamogetse G. Morwe, youth development expert and researcher of student violence at the University of Venda (Univen); and Prof. Thierry Luescher, a higher education researcher at the HSRC and UFS, that the idea of a Photovoice-driven project could be realised. Dr Wilson Fadiji brought with her the expertise in wellbeing studies, while Dr Morwe contributed her expertise in student movement-related violence. The NRF call represented the opportunity to research the 2015/16 student movement further, while adding the new perspective of psychological wellbeing.

By taking a wellbeing approach, we wanted to investigate the strengths and resources that might have been prevalent in the arduous experiences of students in the student movement and the aftermath of exposure to student movement-related violence. The project should be a useful conduit for difficult reflections between student activists; it should also involve Student Affairs practitioners, student counsellors, university leaders, and higher education policy role players.

In the course of 2018, we submitted a proposal to the NRF, and by the end of the year we had received information confirming the success of our application for funding. We had initially designed the study to involve at least one university per province, as well as ensuring variation in terms of different institutional mandates, histories, and localities. However, the final approved funding was limited, hence the need to limit ourselves to five universities. In retrospect, this limitation did not have a negative impact on the project, as the team was of the opinion that after having visited the first four universities, we were now reaching a point of "saturation" in the data; indeed, no new information was emerging by the time of working with the students from the fifth and final institution.

The process of "data gathering" thus focused on five universities in South Africa. They were representative in terms of different types of categorisation: three were historically disadvantaged universities, two were rural universities, one was a university of technology, and one was a merged institution. The five institutions were visited in this order: the University of the Western Cape (2019), the University of Venda (2019), the University of the Free State (2019), the University of Fort Hare (2020) and the Durban University of Technology (2020 via Zoom). The visits were organised as either three-day or four-day workshops and designed to allow for deep engagement with participants. Except in the case of DUT, where we took the methodology online, all workshops were held on the campuses of the universities, face to face with the students. Details of the methodology have been published in the open access article "Rapid Photovoice as a close-up, emancipatory methodology in student experience research: The case of the student movement violence and wellbeing study" (Luescher et al., 2021b) in the prestigious *International Journal of Qualitative Methods*.

In order to ensure that the findings across campuses would be comparable, similar procedures were followed, with adjustments made to suit the demands of students on each campus. Briefly put, engagements with student activists were organised around social media-based exploratory conversations followed by workshops, including an introductory and training session, photo gathering, reflective discussions, and exhibitions. At the end of every session, there was a debriefing meeting allowing the participants to reflect on the processes that had taken place. One aspect of the strategic thinking behind this

project was to ensure that key findings were going to be made available to academics, Student Affairs practitioners, stakeholders in education and other public entities, and the public at large. From the start we were also committed to exploring different and innovative forms of scholarly and cross-over publications to communicate.

By taking a wellbeing approach, we wanted to investigate the strengths and resources that might have been prevalent in the arduous experiences of students in the student movement and the aftermath of exposure to student movement-related violence. The project should be a useful conduit for difficult reflections between student activists; it should also involve Student Affairs practitioners, student counsellors, university leaders, and higher education policy role players.

THE IMPACT OF COVID-19

In the course of the second year of the project, the COVID-19 pandemic and lockdown imposed a travel ban and made it impossible to carry out further in-person, face-to-face workshops. Thus, the research team invested time and effort into producing two scholarly manuscripts. The first, which is currently published as "Rapid Photovoice as a close-up, emancipatory methodology in student experience research: The case of the student movement violence and wellbeing study" (Luescher et al., 2021a), provides a detailed outline of what we termed "a Rapid Photovoice methodology". In this manuscript, we describe the methodological issues associated with doing a Photovoice workshop within a limited time frame. Important ethical issues are raised, as well as reflections of the extent to which such a process can be empowering, emancipatory, and addressing the needs of the study.

In our second manuscript, we apply Lefebvre's concept of "social space" to shed light on the resources, strengths, and indicators of functioning that student activists refer to and discuss in reflecting on student movement activities and their wellbeing impacts. We bring to light what students describe as a resource to them (and how they do this). This particularly when faced with upheavals on campus, violence in the movement, police brutality and brutality from private security services, and a lack of attention from management, and when their education/career becomes precarious as a result of their involvement in the movement's activities. On campuses like UWC and DUT, it was more difficult to identify resources from participants' reports. It would seem like the spaces the students found themselves in were intensely negative, so much so that a wellbeing perspective into their lived experiences was not feasible. Not to say there were no resources at these two sites, but students felt it was better to discuss and grapple with the obvious difficulties faced rather than attempt to find "a flower in the desert". As the narratives included in wellbeing themes like "safe spaces" and "wellbeing" show, activists even from these universities became cognisant of and could articulate their wellbeing resources. Yet, it is also evident from their photographs and reflections that there is a spatial disconnect between their experiences of violence (on campus) and the spatial location of their wellbeing resources (which tend to be off campus).

THE PHOTOGRAPHS

#FeesMustFall and its Aftermath tells the varied stories of the 35 students by using images of their experiences. The majority of these images were not taken by the students at the occasion of the Photovoice workshops. Somewhat contrary to our expectations, the students harvested memories mainly from their online social media archives and their phones and laptops to bring to the workshop sessions photographs that would help them to illustrate and articulate their thoughts.

In over 100 images, the project uncovers the student activists' motivations for engaging in the student movement, their experiences, their journeys, their reflections, and their alternative choices.

THE BOOK AND THE PROJECT

The book presents the majority of the photographs together with related captions and short narratives written by the students during the Photovoice workshops. They are presented in themes that closely resemble, but also go beyond, the travelling and online exhibitions that accompany this book. In addition, the book also documents the methodology used in the research process and includes personal reflections of participants in the project – students, research interns, and administrative and research staff.

Overall, the book *#FeesMustFall and its Aftermath* provides a space for the most comprehensive coverage of the project. We hope that it will provide new understandings of student movement experiences and advance the goals of the project as a whole. The picture-heavy approach is supposed to allow the pictures to drive the narrative within each of the guiding themes. We are hopeful that this book will be useful to student counselling professionals, academic leaders, and student leaders, all of whom certainly care for the wellbeing of students; and to university leaders, security officials, officials in the national higher education department, the minister, their advisors and other policy role players, who have South Africa's and students' best interests at heart.

Beyond the current project and the impact already made from our various outputs, it is our hope that the project reproduces itself into other forms of research that will benefit South African students and the post-schooling education and training sector in general. Reflecting on future projects, we hope to engage further on student wellbeing, using other innovative methodologies.

THE GOALS OF THE PROJECT ARE TO

- expose the unacceptable, high levels of violence on university campuses and the impact this has on student wellbeing.

- create awareness in the public, in government and among higher education policy makers and university leaders to ensure that student grievances are taken seriously without the need for protesting.

- ban riot police and security services from university campuses.

- de-stigmatise student mental health issues at universities.

- expand student counselling services to better support students who struggle with mental health issues.

AFTERMATH
VIOLENCE AND WELLBEING IN THE CONTEXT OF THE STUDENT MOVEMENT

THE ORGANISATION OF THE BOOK

The book is organised as a compilation of several elements. Overall, they make up 18 chapters:

First of all, there are 13 chapters that make up the photo exhibition contained in this book. They present the students' photos with their titles and short reflections, as provided by the student participants. The photos were grouped by the research team into different themes with an added theme descriptor.

The first set of exhibition chapters comprises the following themes:
- A history of struggle (chapter 3),
- Oppressive spaces (chapter 4), and
- The violence of institutions (chapter 5)

The second set of exhibition chapters deals with themes on protesting itself:
- Conscientise and mobilise (chapter 6)
- Protesting and violence (chapter 7)
- Fire (chapter 8)

The third set of photographs is thematised and grouped into chapters as follows:
- Gender inside the movement (chapter 10)
- Fear and trauma (chapter 11)
- Outcomes of protests (chapter 12)

These three sets are more reflective on protesting and violence itself.

They are followed by a final exhibition set which deals with wellbeing and wellbeing resources. The four chapters in this set are thematised as follows:

- Unity and solidarity (chapter 14)
- Wellbeing (chapter 15)
- Escape and safe spaces (chapter 16)
- Movement with a purpose (chapter 17)

Unless otherwise indicated, all the photographs in the book come from the student activists' submissions during the project's Photovoice workshops. In keeping with the Photovoice methodology, the photos, their titles, and their captions and narratives are the means by which the students have reflected on the meaning of their experiences of violence and wellbeing during the 2015/16 #FeesMustMall movement in their own words. Thus, the exhibition can be understood as a way of "presenting the data" in a slightly processed format, that is, ordered and thematised. Each photo goes with a title and a short narrative that provides context for the photo and shows the meaning that the student ascribes to it. Together, the titles, narratives, and pictures tell a vivid story of the violent experiences that students endured during the movement, as well as the wellbeing resources they mobilised to cope with the negative effects of the violence experienced.

The four sets of exhibition chapters are framed by and interspersed with five chapters that deal with aspects of the research project as a whole and of this book in particular.

They start in chapter 1 with our reflections on the problem we sought to investigate and help address with the project, and key quotes that illustrate our understanding of key concepts and our commitments to the wellbeing of South African students. The chapter expresses our hope that with this project, we contribute to a new political culture on university campuses and beyond, and to the provision of higher education that gives all students an equal chance to succeed, so that it may contribute to individual actualisation, collective development, and overall a democratic, free, socially just, and prosperous Africa.

This is followed by chapter 2, which gives an overview of our conceptualisation of the project, the key concepts, and the book. Attention is also drawn to the deliberately contradictory format of the book.

Chapter 9 goes into more detail on our methodology of recruiting former student activists and working with them through a series of workshops, analysing the data and making sense of it, and finally ensuring an ethical and trustworthy process and outcome.

Chapter 13 concludes the discussion of the project-related conceptualisation and process by illustrating ways in which the project is seeking to realise its advocacy and knowledge production goals.

The final chapter, chapter 18, reflects on the contributions of the research project, its main findings to date and its conclusions.

In the appendix, the individual biographies of several research team and project members, including some student participants, are presented. The chapter outlines the contours of a philosophy of violence encapsulated in the students' reflections as well as their complex conceptions of wellbeing.

Overall, we hope that the book is able to contribute to the attainment of the project's goals, which were established, elaborated, and refined in successive Photovoice workshops, along with the modalities by which we aimed to achieve them (see box on page 16).

We are immensely grateful for all the support we received in the process of generating this book, including the words of support and the endorsements in the book's foreword and afterword.

The original goals of the project were revised and amended in the course of the Photovoice workshops with the students to arrive at a set of advocacy goals that are far-reaching and meaningful.

RESTORING
WELLBEING
AFTER STUDENT PROTESTS
LESSONS FROM #FEESMUSTFALL
AND ITS AFTERMATH

Keamogetse G Morwe, Thierry M Luescher and Angelina Wilson Fadiji

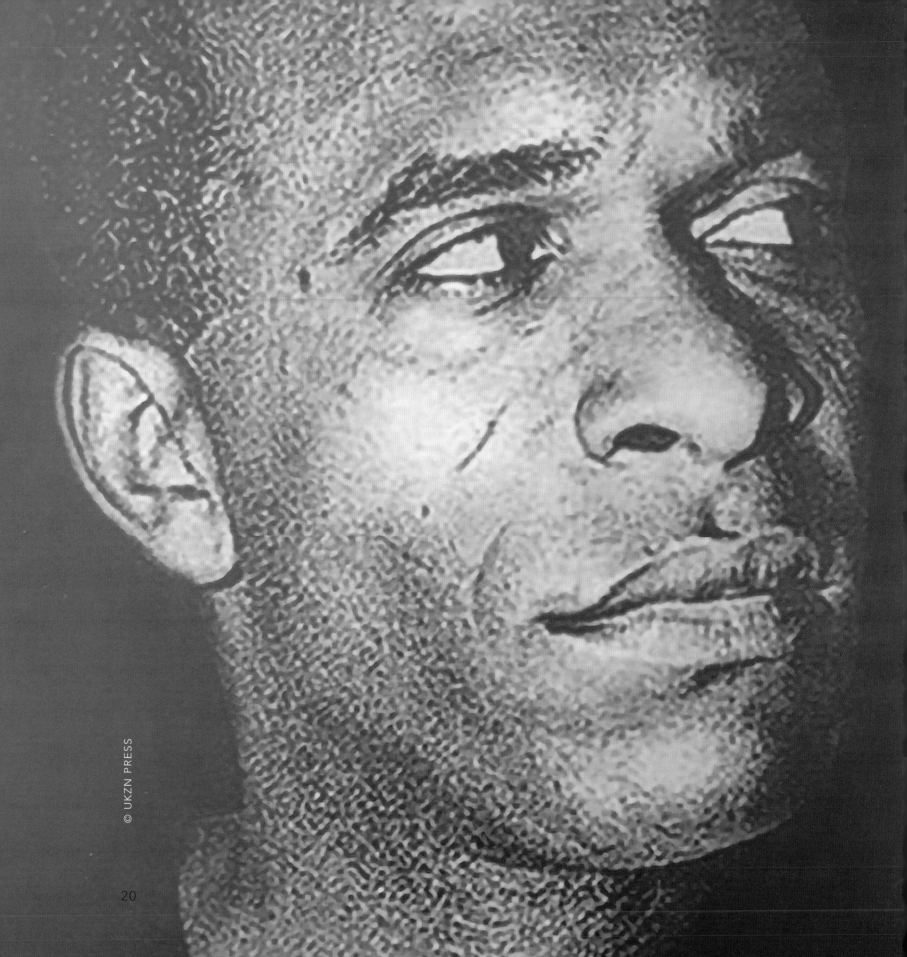

20

CHAPTER 3

A HISTORY OF STRUGGLE

> "
>
> *Each generation must, out of relative obscurity, discover its mission, fulfil it, or betray it. (Fanon, 1961)*
>
> "

Many of the demands that students made and the issues that students raised during the #FeesMustFall protests in 2015/16 had been brewing for many years prior and were widely acknowledged as legitimate (Jansen, 2017; Habib, 2019). The #FeesMustFall campaign that started in September 2015 at Wits University was not an isolated event. There had been student protests for years, carried out mainly by black students at historically black universities, and the student leaders in the #FeesMustFall protests were aware of this history (Jacobs, 2015; Luescher et al., 2020).

There had also been a wave of protests mainly at historically white universities in the same year, starting with #RhodesMustFall at UCT, and followed by #OpenStellenbosch and other campus-based mobilisations, which dealt with matters the students broadly conceived as

"decolonisation" and which #FeesMustFall picked up and incorporated. The very name #FeesMustFall was inspired by these earlier campus-specific movements.

The two pictures and narratives included under the theme "A history of struggle" capture an even broader awareness of history: that there had been previous youth and student protestors who served as inspiration and a source of pride for the generation of student activists of 2015/16. A quote from Frantz Fanon's seminal work *The Wretched of the Earth* provided inspiration and motivation for many student activists, who mentioned this repeatedly in our Photovoice workshops:

"Each generation must, out of relative obscurity, discover its mission, fulfil it, or betray it" (Fanon, 1990 [1961], p. 166).

CONNECTING WITH THE ANCESTORS

Akhona Manyenyeza, UFH

This picture was taken on the 24th of February 2019. This photo shows a former student leader, who used to give direction to the student masses on how to deal with issues that affect them peacefully. The photo was taken at Sobukwe House that is an office of PASMA (Pan Africanist Student Movement of Azania) at the University of Fort Hare (UFH) (Alice campus). The office used to be an office where PASMA members used to cluster together to discuss the issues that affect students under the banner of high morality and high discipline. I was sitting there and remembering how the issues affecting students used to be addressed without violence.

WHO WOULD HAVE THOUGHT? (1976 RELOADED)

Sphelele Khumalo, UWC

Young, old,

Black and white,

Rich and poor,

The oppressor and the oppressed,

Who would have thought that the bomb was to explode,

Post 25+ years of fallacious democracy,

The centre can no longer hold,

State violence re-activated,

Black bodies on the line again,

Back at the gates of 1976 student protest, aren't we?

The lullness of 1994 politics can no longer pass unchallenged!

We move past the Mandela Dream,

Hopefully Biko, Sobukwe, Sankara, Cabral, Garvey are ready for us,

Long live the Spirit of 1976! Long life!

WHITE STAND _VIOLENT SYMBOLISM

Kamohelo Maphike, UFS

This picture is a symbolic sight of uninterrupted white hegemony, racism, and an extreme attitude of symbolic anti-blackness. The opening sentence is justified by understanding Maphike (2018:5), [who says] that symbols in any society are attached to values, representation, art, and a celebration of history. The symbol presented in this picture presents a false sense of white purity and a superiority mentality encompassed by both white students and white members of staff. According to Maphike (2018: 5), such symbols are viewed as "territorial symbols". Territorial symbols are normally built to mark a territory of a particular group, celebrating victory over a dominated group etc. The statute of Steyn is a reminder that RACIST AFRIKANER NATIONALISM reigns supreme in this university. Moreover, it articulates an artistic meaning that this space was not meant for people of colour. A violent articulation.

CHAPTER 4

OPPRESSIVE SPACES

> **"**
>
> *Student activists focus attention on the continued glorification of the oppressor, colonialism, and apartheid on university campuses. They illustrate and name everyday encounters with racism and patriarchy as they manifest in university campus spaces.*
>
> **"**

The meaning and significance of space in the transformation of higher education has been highlighted in the work of Philippa Tumubweinee with her research on the campus of UFS. At the same time, the student movement starting with #RhodesMustFall at UCT ever so articulately pointed to the need to decolonise campus space, living and learning, and culture and knowledge in South African universities universities. They did so inspired by overseas student movements linked to #BlackLivesMatter and #BlackOnCampus as well as campaigns like Oxford University's #RhodesMustFall and Harvard Law Schools' #RoyallMustFall.

"Space is not the void between brick and mortar; neither is it an abstract thing that is independent of the substantial social relations within it. Rather, (social) space, in the original of Lefebvre and others building on him, is a (social) product, which co-produces the social nature of institutions such as universities. This reading of space as social also involves the political, because social space is where 'the struggles and contradictions of 'living actuality' (Kipfer, 2009: xxi) happen'. Against this reading of space, the reality of everyday student life on campus, […] is therefore a co-construct between human actors and the space within which they act and relate." (Tumubweinee & Luescher, 2019, p. 2).

With photos and narratives that have been grouped under the theme "Oppressive spaces", student activists focus attention on the continued glorification of the oppressor, colonialism, and apartheid on university campuses. They illustrate and name everyday encounters with racism and patriarchy as they manifest in university campus spaces. Thus, the student activists illustrate students' experiences which they are not able to ignore and willing to give into, which is part of the motive for students to join the student movement.

ALTERNATIVE DISSENT

Anonymous, UFS

This image affirms to me that expressing dissent and injustice can take various modes of expression. The bureaucracy of the institution forces legitimacy onto only formalised modes of engagement such as dialogues, negotiations, mediation, and protests they have given permission for. These modes are ineffective and are often swallowed up and erased by the bureaucracy. New forms of expression and dissent need to be explored and utilised.

This image also reminds me, through the presence of my friends arm in the corner of the frame, of the personal sacrifice others made to assist me in putting the pictures up. People can collectively come together to rectify injustice and that when they do, personal sacrifice becomes less important than collective gain. [This is] taken from personal archives on 1 April 2019, to protest against the ineffective implementation of the UFS sexual harassment policy.

UNIVERSITY OF THE UNFREE STATE

Anonymous, UFS

We will never forget the brutalities of the #ShimalsParkIncident. This eruption followed a few years later after the #ReitzIncident, which the institution failed to address thoroughly [...] instead opting for a very cosmetic approach.

This university is deeply embedded in racism and racial inequality. The protest was never meant to be violent but because when we challenge the space we are directly confronting privilege, the white students had to defend what they hold dear, a rugby match, over the lives of black students and workers who are affected by the violent systematic inequalities.

DEAR WHITE PEOPLE
LEFT, Anonymous, UFS

... particularly the cishet white conservative men, this is a love letter from a mourning and revolting black queer woman. WE BELONG HERE. F*ck You!

THE INVISIBLE GATES
RIGHT, Tshepo Raseala, Univen

The phrase "fences are meant to either keep people in or out" reflects our views of the university's concrete palisade fence in times of protest actions. In fear of being kept out by the fence, the first thing that students do when protests action commences is to open impromptu "gates" by breaking down the palisades from the fence.

This allows students to find easier access to the Riverside residence on campus as compared to having to run to the main gate which would increase chances of the police catching-up with the protesters.

The name was chosen because as much as the "gates" are there during the protests, they are invisible (not there or not accessible) in peaceful or regular times.

RAPE OF BLACK WOMXN: THE EYE OF THE STORM, A BLACK BODY

Anonymous, UFS

This image is of a building that bears the name of an apartheid scientist who created biological warfare tools and contraceptives that were forcefully injected into the bodies of Black womxn when they were appointed as labourers in industries and factories. There has been no movement to change the name of this building.

This speaks to the specific social standpoint that Black womxn occupy in South Africa, and the concentrated warfare conducted on their bodies continuously throughout history. Other struggles, the names of other buildings and other statues have taken preference over this one. No discussion has been formed around this one because it seems as though society is invested in erasing the violence that is a dominant theme of a Black womxn's livelihood. [This is] taken from personal archives on 21 October in preparation for this project.

[Editorial note: The apartheid scientist who created biological warfare tools that Anonymous has in mind is actually "Dr Wouter Basson" also known as "Dr Death". Wynand Mouton whom the UFS theatre building is named after was an academic, rector, and eventually chancellor of the university].

Unit for institutional change

A PRICE FOR THE REALISATION OF SOCIAL JUSTICE "HERE"; DO WE EVEN DESERVE JUSTICE? OR MAYBE "JUST ICE"!

Tshepang Mahlatsi, UFS

What is seen here is a sign of what was then the Institute for Reconciliation and Social Justice during 2015/16, now called the Unit for Institutional Change and Social Justice. Every day on my way to campus I always pass this sign and every day I am reminded how violent this space is and how every time a black body at this institution needs to be put on the line, before a step is taken to address the subtle structural inequalities. [The] Reitz Incident, Shimla Park Incident, Tswelopele Incident, and other racial incidents reported and others not reported serve as a reminder that black bodies here will always pay a price for social justice. We all play the victims of the violence of 2015/16 but a black body felt it physically and emotionally and will never recover!

DEFENDING CAMPUS AT GOLGATHA

This picture is part of the Univen collage of pictures that was submitted by Kulani Mlambo without further caption. It depicts students who shield themselves behind a felled tree and sheets of zinc from rubber bullets shot at them by the police. The students shut down the university and barricaded the access street at Golgatha bridge so as to prevent university staff or police from entering.

CHAPTER 5

THE VIOLENCE OF INSTITUTIONS

In his essay "Lenin and Philosophy", French sociologist Louis Althusser conceptualised two types of state institutions. Ideological state apparatuses (ISA) such as educational and religious institutions, he argued, operated by methods of ideology. Repressive state apparatuses (RSA) such as the courts, police, and prisons, used physical violence to achieve the goal of domination (Althusser, 1970). As ideological state apparatuses, universities operate by a diversity of practices and rituals, which produce particular responses by humans, and these roles or subject positions that humans take on are the lived experience of ideology. On the whole, the task of ISA is to ultimately reproduce the ruling ideology, which is always an ideology of domination, so as to provide a "glue" for, or cement the totality of social relations (Althusser, 1970, pp. 141-144; Giddens, 1977, p. 179).

The theme "The violence of institutions" captures a rupture in the functioning of South Africa's public universities as ISA. Universities operations, which are experienced as violent, produce an emancipatory and frequently violent response by students, and in turn, prompt the universities (with court interdicts and private security) and the state to mobilise RSA to counteract the student protests. The cycle of violence and repression that this produces is well studied and known to create a culture of violence in student activism (Nkomo, 1984; Altbach, 1991; Luescher, 2018; Morwe, 2021). What this theme chiefly presents is pictures that show how the same institutions that are entrusted by the people to emancipate and empower young people can end up in a contradictory position where they become the antithesis of their own *raison d'être* by shutting off engagement and repressing critical dissent. If, as Madonsela (2021) suggests in the quote presented in chapter 1, there were adult men and women leading the institutions of the state, leaders who can sit down, listen, and get transformation done, there was no need for stun grenades and rubber bullets on university campuses.

What this theme chiefly presents is pictures that show how the same institutions that are entrusted by the people to emancipate and empower young people can end up in a contradictory position.

PEOPLE!!! PEOPLE!! NOT STONES!!!!!

Anonymous, UFS

We always have to remind the institution that they are dealing with people and not just objects that are moving around the space with no sense of belonging and feeling. We are people, human beings, not just things you can call the police on and militarise the space every time we demonstrate our discontent.

OUR BODIES ARE NOT DISPOSABLE!!

BOILING

Blessing Mavhuru, Univen

This photo points to boiling emotions through [the] pains of inequality and uncertainty [about] the future. The present is painful but [the] future is dark, blind, and dry. Boiling and [an] increase in temperature fuels the struggles of students.

OUT OF POWER BUT NOT OUT OF RESPONSIBILITY

Siphephelo (Shange) Mthembu, DUT

This picture represents victimisation, such as financial exclusion and academic exclusion, that comes with being a student activist in an institution of higher learning. It also carries with it a lot of emotion because directing students and trying to assist them in a brutalising system when I have also been a victim of the system was not easy. Despite my own challenges, I could not run away from my leadership responsibilities, and I had to help lead students in the right direction.

THE STATE OF IZWELETHU

Siyasanga Ndwayi, UWC

In the picture, I am in a police truck. I am shouting through the window. We were arrested in Parliament for protesting with pensioners who wanted their money from the government since the 1980s. In the truck I was with three elders and my close comrade, Zwai Zazi.

I've titled it "The state of izwelethu" due to the fact that it depicts how we are treated in our land and the amount of violence young black people [have been subjected to], including our grandparents.

QUEST FOR DECOLONIALITY: AGAINST ALL ODDS

Sphelele Khumalo, UWC

The photo presented symbolises how the state was determined by all means necessary to halt student protests. A one-way approach employed at all cost. The ANC government continues to play the middle in blocking the realisation of total emancipation for the oppressed in favour of those who continue to rule this stolen country. A neo-liberal state at all times ready and prepared to protect the interest of capital even by means of violence.

This photo is taken at the peak of the protests and shows the delegitimisation of student protests through violence employed and [the] militarisation of academic spaces. If something changed in 1994, fokol changed!

45

THE BATTLE OF LIBERTY OR THE EPITOME OF VIOLENCE?

Siyasanga Ndwayi, UWC

The police and private security were attacking us in residences. This was next to the Liberty Residence, hence we called it "The battle of Liberty".

The picture depicts the epitome of state violence and how we were forced to retaliate using dust bins to shield ourselves. It was on 11 November 2015 during the #FeesWillFall protests. Pastor Xola Skosana wrote a beautiful piece on this day.

47

SPIRIT OF UNWANTED PEACE

Dimakatso Ngobeni, Univen

This picture was taken in August 2018 during the 225 Strike. The students were fighting police, and the police chased the students up until they pushed them where they are staying in the res. These are the residences where disabled students are staying (between F3 male res and F4 for females). In the picture we see students are using two dustbins to close the road for the police hippo not to pass. There is teargas coming out of the entrance of the residence; the residence has a turnstile gate that needs a student card, and the police were unable to get in, so they threw teargas through the gate.

Looking at this picture makes me sad. When I am thinking of the students who are disabled, they cannot be helped by anyone in this situation. They are more affected than us who caused the strike. In those two residences we have blind people and those who are using wheelchairs; others who have asthma, they can lose their life; and other who are bipolar, they can be traumatised.

NO RETREAT, NO SURRENDER

Abednego Sam Mandhlazi, Univen

No retreat is a military word that means without giving up or retiring.

The comrades and students in the picture are our forces. They were fighting the police regardless of the unfavourable conditions.

KEEPING UP WITH THE KOMRADES

Ncedisa Bemnyama, UWC

We had become the Kardashians of the movement, and we used to make fun of this, that we are now the popular people – the Popstars of the Struggle – that comrades love and despise [all] at once.

This picture was taken in Cape Town. Some old ANC stalwarts wanted to talk to us and co-opt us and they took us to hotels not to be seen by the media. For instance we met Pallo Jordan. In the picture here, we had taken a break from deliberations. I am standing at the back. Some of my friends here are from Black Land First (BLF), others from PASMA and one Economic Freedom Fighters (EFF). The comrades in question are Ntokozo, Phethani, Lindokuhle, Mandisi, and Mokgweetsi.

BETRAYAL OF HOPE

Xola Zatu, UFS

As trees epitomise hope and bring life – the bright sun imparting joy... The shade engraved depicts how rigid the system is and its brutality against student activists. This picture was taken at UFS, Bloemfontein Campus on 21 October 2019.

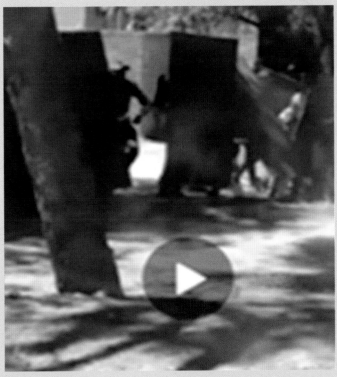

STRATEGIC RETALIATION

Litha Dyomfana, UFH

The picture reflects [the] events of the first strike of the 2020 academic year. When students engage with police, the police come with firearms, teargas, and rubber bullets, making it an unfair fight with students. It is a one-sided fight because it is not realistic to fight a gun with a stone. It shows how students stand-up for themselves even though it is losing the battle. The students are forced to carve out resources instead of dangerous weapons. It brings a feeling of hope and solidarity as students find ways to effectively combat the police.

It shows unity, oneness, mission, and goals where students fight collectively. It is the only time students have the same vision

CHAPTER 6
CONSCIENTISE AND MOBILISE

According to Donatella della Porta and Mario Diani, "social movements are a distinct social process, consisting of the mechanisms through which actors engage in collective action; are involved in conflictual relations which clearly identify opponents; are linked by dense informal networks; [and] share a distinct collective identity" (2006, p. 20, our emphasis). The idea of a collective identity involves that:

"Social movements are not merely the sum of protest events on certain issues, or even of specific campaigns. On the contrary, a social movement process is in place only when collective identities develop, which go beyond specific events and initiatives. Collective identity is strongly associated with recognition and the creation of connectedness (Pizzorno, 1996). It brings with it a sense of common purpose and shared commitment to a cause, which enables single activists and/or organisations to regard themselves as inextricably linked to other actors, not necessarily identical but surely compatible, in a broader collective mobilisation (Touraine, 1981)." (Della Porta & Diani, 2006, p. 21).

A "sense of common purpose" and a "shared commitment to a cause" do not emerge without the hard work of movement intellectuals who elaborate the movement ideology and spread it. In the case of #FeesMustFall, the "fallist" ideology elaborated first by #RhodesMustFall activists was founded on three pillars: Pan Africanism, Black Radical Feminism and Black Consciousness. As Rekgotsofetse Chikane (2018) shows, fellow student activists would meet in groups to educate one another on these pillars of thought to foster a sense of unity.

MOBILISE, EDUCATE, & STRIVE

Asandiswa Bomvana, UWC

This picture was taken at Reslife Center at UWC in 2016 during the #FeesWillFall campaign. This is where we would organise ourselves and sharpen any contradictions we had before we go out and face the enemy. It is where we built our momentum and [the] unity amongst us. It is very critical for us to organise ourselves and conscientise within.

BLACK HOUSE COLLECTIVE FAMILY

Azania Simthandile Tyhali, UWC

The picture was taken at the Black House Collective in Joburg. I make mention of this space because it resembled a black space we had imagined.

This was a depressing time, for many cadres in this picture were expelled from the ivory towers. Here we had come to regroup [with] other forces from Johannesburg whom we had created and with whom we had political relations.

Here we had a braai and a visit from Nelson Maldonado Torres, a decolonial scholar from Puerto Rico, and Umrabulo sessions.

THE FOCAL POINT OF CONSCIENTISATION

Siyasanga Ndwayi, UWC

We were in the TV room of Cassinga residence at UWC. I was facilitating a political ed.

This is where we were able to politicise and educate one another in relation to decolonisation. In this session I was tasked to speak on Pan Africanism. My talk was based on Kwame Ture.

60

CHAPTER 7

PROTEST AND VIOLENCE

This theme shows the extent to which the student protests were engulfed by the spell of violence, exerted by students, police, and security services. Numerous pictures that were volunteered by the student activists depict moments of protest action. Some show the painful consequences of physical violence such as the pictures of students' gashing bullet wounds. When talking about the pictures, students often reflected on the unnecessary violence that would take place at protests. Frequently, the activists would argue that violence was initiated by police and security personnel and forced students to retaliate. Many of the case studies in Malose Langa's (2017) analysis of #FeesMustFall concur with this view. The theme also touches on the dynamics that existed between the larger student body that did not want to partake in the movement and student activists. At times, students would be coerced to attend mass meetings organised by student activists and cajoled into participating in marches. Overall, what is missing in the depictions of protesting is the novel online dimension that made the #FeesMustFall protests unique in democratic South Africa. The use of social media, chiefly Twitter, Facebook, and WhatsApp groups, enabled speedy and cross-campus communication and mobilisation. It also provided a mechanism for getting the students' message into the public media, mobilising public support, and thus pressing students' onto the political agenda (Satgar in Booysen, 2016; Bosch et al., 2020; Luescher et al., 2021a).

DEFENCE MECHANISM

Kulani Mlambo, Univen

This was our source of strength. We did not have guns; we had to protect our self with stones; this was our shield, our protection; this was a constant reminder that a black student has to fight to break the shackles of academic chains; as we threw each and every stone; we saw ourselves getting closer to our freedom; when the police ran away from the stones, it was a sign that we are making a valid statement to everyone. However, it was painful to see ourselves fighting for academic freedom while other students from the A-class were receiving everything on a silver platter; they have never fought for anything; they had never had a reason to protest as if the country belonged to them. As for the black student, everything had to be war, fights, and violence. We never lost hope, because we knew that we were fighting a just cause; we were ready for anything, because we wanted to save a black child's future; we didn't have proper fighting materials; we only had stones – stones inside a trolley.

RESPONSE

Asandiswa Bomvana, UWC

This picture was taken at UWC in 2015 during the #FeesWillFall campaign. Songezo is holding up the cardboard with Bongo next to him. For me the cardboard shows the true narrative how it was; it is a true eye-opener. Ours was that we were responding to the violence, we were retaliating, not the other way around.

WALK FOR A JUST CAUSE

Sphelele Khumalo, UWC

Sometimes the oppressed give in to their oppression and internalise their sufferings. In the moment of internalising the sufferings, one then further disallows themselves any thought that may speak to the end of their suffering. The 2015/16 student protests, like any other revolt against oppression, was not without pushback. Lo and behold, some of that pushback came from the oppressed that the movement rallied for. This is telling of how deep the oppression goes; also, it is revealing in how it has managed to create a self-reproducing machine that is well protected by its very victims.

This constantly led to the need for us, protesting students, to always make it clear why we were protesting, what our demands were and importantly, why the movement was not just an unfortunate event of our time but a discourse towards the fulfilment of our generational mission, as the great thinker Frantz Fanon would have it. Black young generation standing firm. Enough is enough!

CIRCLE OF STRUGGLE

Siphephelo (Shange) Mthembu, DUT

This picture describes the instigation of violence; those carrying the sticks are intimidating those who don't want to participate in the protest.

We were disrupting classes so that we could mobilise students to take part in the protest.

We also wanted to make sure that students that were still attending classes, because they had the money to pay for their fees, were not able to continue to do so. This was to ensure that the disadvantaged students that were taking part in the protests would not be compromised academically, while the privileged students were going on as normal.

MBAYI-MBAYI

Azania Simthandile Tyhali, UWC

This was outside Parliament in 2016 while waiting for cadres. In this picture, I am singing "Guerilla asikwazi ubaleka". This song for us was informed by and was a response to police brutality and how they violently brutalised us, both at the institution and outside. These were the times of spontaneous hyper-politics.

CALM BEFORE THE STORM

Siphelele Mancobeni, UFH

This picture was taken in 2017 close by the UFH Admin Building. This was the first student strike we had with the new vice-chancellor, Prof. Buhlungu, in place. Already at his inauguration, we disturbed the function because we wanted meal allowances. The strike addressed this, and there were also other demands. I took this picture to remind me of the strike which was also the first encounter we had as students with Xhobani security company. We were scared of them because they were bulky and fit; before it was always SAPS. I was a third year student then.

THE RETURN

Hlulani C. Chabalala, Univen

Two boys holding the teargas. This shows [the] pain that we feel when the police throw teargas [at] our students. In return, they must feel it. It emphasises the resistance of students towards the management and the police.

NO VIP IN THE REVOLUTION

Hlulani C. Chabalala, Univen

There was a student residence called Riverside that was full of teargas smoke. Riverside is the residence where postgraduates stay. In the 2017 march, the Univen students embarked on a strike. The purpose of the strike was to address NSFAS (National Student Financial Aid Scheme) allowances. This march was called the 225 movement. While other students were on the streets, the Riverside students stayed in their rooms because they felt they were not affected. In return, they faced a huge challenge of teargas being thrown in their rooms.

CAUSALITY OF THE REVOLUTION

Bob Sandile Masango, Univen

With this photo, I reflect on the revolutionary support I get from my family, comrades, and friends after being brutalised by the police, arrested, and detained for seven days in prison without medical attention in 2017.

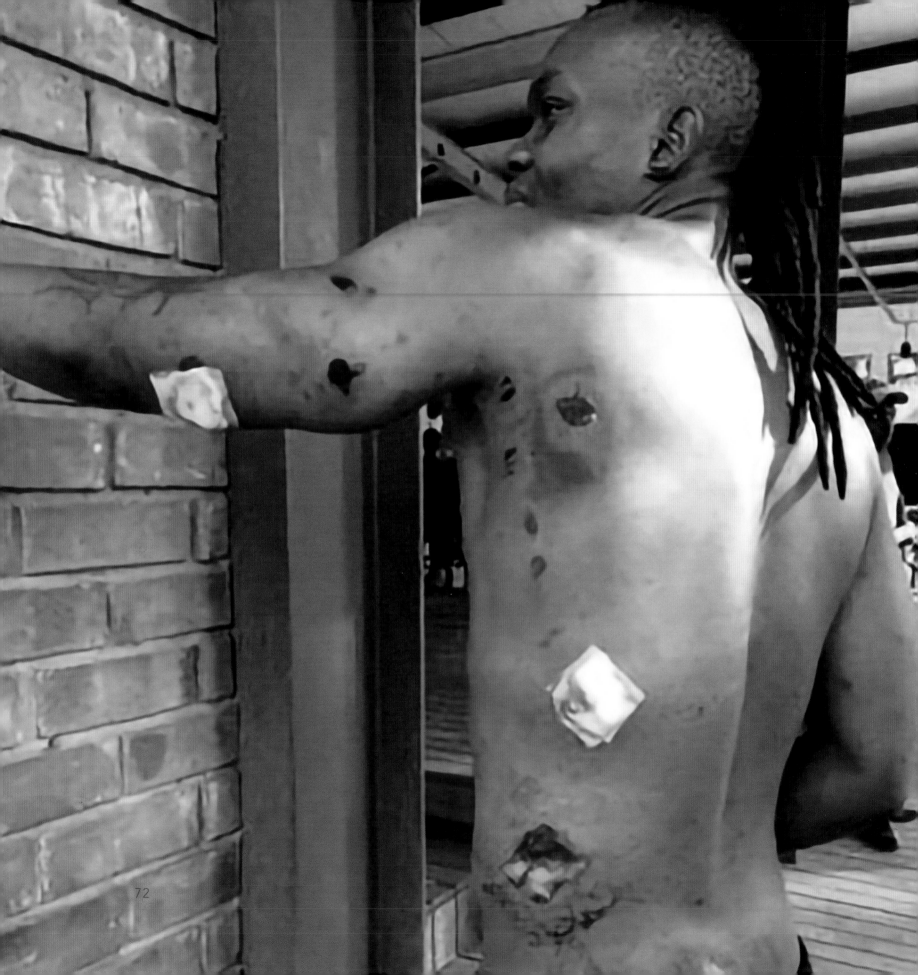

72

MANDLA TIBANE

Bob Sandile Masango, Univen

This is a photo of a late close friend and comrade of mine who was brutally attacked by police.

After the brutalising treatment, he was badly injured. The police still detained him for no reason.

He was about to register for a PhD but because the universities are anti-black, his life was shortened and he died having a pending case.

I remember how we struggled to raise money to pay lawyers after the charges were fabricated against us.

EMSINI

Siyasanga Ndwayi, UWC

We were protesting at Rondebosch Police Station against the victimisation of our comrades, Mlandu and Slovo, who were expected to turn themselves in on that day in relation to their #FeesMustFall activities at UCT. Without lawyers or any form of legal representation, we decided to take it to the streets and protest. We were Emsini, which means we were at war.

FEARLESS GENERATION

Lesley Ngazire, DUT

This picture shows a group of students protesting against academic exclusions. I chose this picture because it is a symbol of unity between the different political parties; South African Students Congress (SASCO), African National Congress Youth League (ANCYL) and the Young Leaders Council (YCL) and the general students who were concerned with the fees and exclusion at residences. The picture shows unity for a common purpose.

#SHACKVILLE PROTESTS AT UCT

The burning of UCT artworks by student activists during the #Shackville protests on 16 February 2016 caused an outcry in South African media. However, according to Nomusa Makhubu (2020, p. 518), in order to understand Shackville, it must be placed "in the postcolonial, post-apartheid South African art context ... as a collective response to the racially segregated visual landscape in South Africa". She continues: "In my view, Shackville, rather than the burnt commissioned portraits and paintings, is the art and the monument we should be paying attention to in understanding the imperial ruination it represents."

©ASHRAF HENDRICKS

CHAPTER 8

FIRE

> "
>
> *Fire can be used for many purposes: to create a focal point for gathering the protesters and calling others from afar; as a weapon to destory, terrorise and bring about chaos.*
>
> "

In *Reflections of South African Student Leaders, 1994 – 2017*, the authors argue that one of the discontinuities in South African student political culture was the extent to which it had become radicalised. They note: "if in the early 1990s littering on campus was considered a radical act of political protest and defiance, by the mid-2010s, the calling nature of fire had become one of the primary ways to gain the attention of an increasingly leaderless and unresponsive political class and university leadership" (Luescher et al., 2020, p. 280). In student protests, fire can be used for many purposes: to create a focal point for gathering the protesters and calling others from afar; as a weapon to destroy, terrorise and bring about chaos; or as a hearth to repose next to, have fellowship and tell stories. This theme brings together various pictures that depict fire in the student movement protests and looks into the use of fire, both physical and symbolic.

LAVUTHA IBHAYI

Litha Dyomfana, UFH

This picture was taken on the 24th of February 2020 during the strike on the UFH Alice campus. The picture shows that the students are ready for anything that will happen. It also shows that there will be light tomorrow. Things will not be like this forever.

It also shows that students could have destroyed university property but they chose not to because they value the university, while the university does not prioritise them as the primary stakeholders of the institution. It shows the love the university students have for the university. They could have destroyed existing infrastructure but because they know what they will benefit from it, they decided not to.

There were over 1000 protesters, however, no university facility was affected.

SYMBOLIC BRAAI TIME

Bob Sandile Masango, Univen

This photo symbolises all protest, which led to a no-fee increment and the dismantling of the middle-man (sBux system) who used to fail to load student allowances in time. Today we are very happy that all students have access and there is no middle-man in the process of paying allowances. We get our money straight from the university when we go to the bank.

IN UNITY WE STAND

Hlulani C. Chabalala, Univen

When students embark on a strike, the first thing they do is to burn things in order to send the message to other students who are still in their rooms. In this picture the tyre is being burned.

This picture also shows students wearing difference political regalia in the protest. This emphasises that when student go to the street for protest, all organisations stand to be united and talk one language for students. When political organisations become one thing, this puts the pressure onto the police and management to respond to the students' demand in time. [The] unity of students makes me feel good because when we demand service delivery from the management, they respond in time.

MATTHEW 3:11 AFTERMATH OF PROTESTS: GOD'S SPACE QUESTIONED

Sphelele Khumalo, UWC

The resistance movement has been present in the country for years. It had people who come from various sectors of life. The church then has been a space for soul healing and building. Now it's the 21st century and student protests are at their peak. The question arises; who is with us?

A church burnt at the CPUT (Cape Town Campus) now drifts the question further. What is the role of the church in our quest for true humanity? When violence has been declared by a state against its people even the house of God is not safe. Either align with the revolution or face with the aftermath of Matthew 3:11. Black theology then becomes an answer to us.

THE "AFTERMATH" EXHIBITION AT STELLENBOSCH UNIVERSITY

In order to create a platform to advocate for the goals of the project, the research team produced a virtual exhibition hosted by South African History Online as well as a physical exhibition which has been travelling from campus to campus and to public sites. It engages various public groups on the study by means of accompanying events. A pilot of this exhibition circus was run in April 2021, hosted by the Stellenbosch University (SU) Museum and the Division for Student Affairs.

CHAPTER 9
OUR METHODOLOGY

> **"**
>
> *One way of empowering people to think critically about their communities and start having conversations about social and political issues that affect their day to day lives is the visual image.*
>
> **"**

In this chapter, we provide a detailed description of the research activities of the study. Within the confines of qualitative research designs, a number of complementary methods were used, including Photovoice, in-depth qualitative research interviews, and the World Café method. We discuss the process of recruiting participants, followed by conducting Photovoice workshops, in-depth interviews, and World Café sessions, the collective analysis of the photos and interpretation of submissions, and finally the ethical implications and ways of ensuring the trustworthiness of the process, findings, and conclusions.

FINDING STUDENTS TO PARTICIPATE IN THE STUDY

Given the sensitive nature of the study, the process of finding participants was not "one size fits all". Recruitment strategies included snowballing, consulting the list of student activists from previous research, and simply going online and reaching out to student leaders. For instance, in the case of UWC, we started recruitment by consulting the list of student activists who formed part of the larger HSRC student movement project (cf. chapter 2). However, for the actual study, we had to use a snowballing technique because none of the students who indicated interest actually showed up on the first day of Photovoice workshops. The only participant who did show up had to assist with referring us to other student activists who agreed to participate in the study. A similar pattern of snowballing took place at Univen.

At UFH, we had obtained a list of student activists, reached out to them and obtained their consent to participate in the study. However, on the day of the workshop, all participants were late for the session. Furthermore, out of the six participants we expected to be part of the workshops, only three of them were eventually available because there were student protests taking place. The team eventually spent the first hour of the session attempting to use snowballing to recruit additional students.

One institution that worked perfectly was UFS. Most of the participants were recruited by emailing student leaders on the UFS website. Almost all of them responded to the email and were present at the workshop itself.

The most difficult and eventually least successful case was DUT, where out of six participants who agreed to participate in the study, only two were available for the full online Photovoice sessions throughout, and another two were available for an individual telephonic interview. The rest failed to show up for various reasons. As mentioned in Chapter 2, COVID-19 impacted the most on the DUT Photovoice plans.

Although we initially envisaged that we would select about 12 students per institution, only Univen and UFS came close to this number. In other institutions, an average of six participants were available for the workshop, which turned out to be an ideal number for our purposes.

In looking for students to participate in the study, we were interested in ensuring an overall representation of the larger student population in terms of gender, race, home language, political affiliation, and year of study. However, given that snowballing became the predominant recruitment method, it became challenging to ensure representativeness. In terms of race, the sample comprised predominantly black Africans. There was some mix of gender, with women making up almost a third (10) of the total sample of 35 student participants (excluding the three master's interns on the project, who were all women). There was an encouraging diversity in home language backgrounds and educational levels, which included both undergraduate and postgraduate students.

DOING PHOTOVOICE

Photovoice is an action research methodology that allows a community to use photographs to document issues that are important to the community, and then select an environment (e.g., a workshop, focus group, or individual interview setting) to discuss these matters, represent them, and ultimately improve the community (Wang & Burris, 1997). The Brazilian intellectual Paulo Freire (2000), from whom the method stems, argued that one way of empowering people to think critically about their communities and start having conversations about social and political issues that affect their day to day lives is the visual image. Thus, Photovoice builds on this idea of empowering people to think critically about their communities and start having conversations about social and political issues that affect their day to day lives, using photos created by research participants themselves (Wang & Burris 1997:370). It thereby empowers community members to record and analyse the status quo and changes in their communities in the language of pictures.

In this project, we attempted to refine this research method and developed what we termed "Rapid Photovoice" (RPV), so called because the time frame for in-person introductions, training, data gathering, discussion and reflection, and an initial presentation of the results, is contracted into four days. Other projects that use Photovoice ordinarily take anywhere from a week to several months for the same process (e.g., Kessi & Cornell, 2015). RPV, in contrast, compresses the core of the data gathering and discussion process into a continuous, intensive three-day series of ten sessions of collective immersion and individual and collective reflection, including a World Café session with external participants on the last day (see Luescher et al., 2021b).

After successfully recruiting a group of student participants on each campus, we emailed each participant a concise and well-designed guide that contained all the information on the project at a glance, including the preliminary goals and proposed process of RPV, the ethics of photography, Photovoice ground rules and guidelines, and a schedule of the sessions (i.e., the activities, workshops, and discussions) that we would hold during the research team's visit to the campus (see Luescher et al., 2021b, for the full description of the daily sessions).

The methodology enabled students to reflect on their traumatic experiences, as well as the wellbeing resources and coping strategies that had been developed in response, in a safe space. (Luescher et al., 2021b, p. 13).

ONLINE RAPID PHOTOVOICE

Data gathering on one of our campuses coincided with the nationwide lockdown resulting from the COVID-19 pandemic. As a result, we had to move RPV online. We designed it to follow the in-person RPV sessions, not bearing in mind the constraints of the virtual space. The first day comprised training in doing Photovoice, as well as discussions of the key research questions, such as the students' involvement in the movement, the role of the violence that occurred during the #FeesMustFall movement on campus, and the resources used to process and cope with the violence. The second day of the online RPV involved the process of photo selection, reflections on the choice and meaning of the photographs, and labelling the photos. We concluded on the third day with a Zoom-hosted Photovoice exhibition. Although it was not the same as an in-person exhibition, participants were still grateful for an opportunity to speak to the collective work they had produced on the issues of violence and wellbeing in the context of the student movement.

THE PROCESS OF DOING RESEARCH INTERVIEWS

Individual interviews were also employed in our interactions with students. These one-on-one conversations were designed as add-ons and follow-ups for students who preferred to share certain aspects of their experiences outside the main workshop.

These interviews were used to explore deeper individual experiences of violence, as well as the resources drawn upon during these difficult experiences to restore wellbeing. We should point out that most participants preferred and enjoyed sharing their experience during the Photovoice workshops.

WORLD CAFE WORKSHOPS

World Café is a participatory research method that seeks to move beyond problem solving and blame assigning, towards learning from what currently works well (Cooperrider & Whitney, 1999). This method places emphasis on how people view the world and how this can be changed through structured discussions. A World Café workshop typically involves setting the context of the session by clarifying the purpose of the dialogue, creating a hospitable space, and then exploring questions that matter through collective attention and collaborative engagement. This method was particularly useful in this study because it enabled the researchers not only to tackle the problem of violence, but also to investigate coping resources for wellbeing as well as ways to mitigate further instigations of violence in higher institutions of learning. A manual for Student Affairs practitioners was produced from this workshop as a tool to discuss ways of preventing violence and restoring student wellbeing in the aftermath of protest violence (see Morwe et al., 2022).

The three methods were complementary, and their respective strengths were geared towards addressing different objectives of the study. All three methods involved much more than a research team coming to collect data from students on a university campus. As the research participants reflections in the Appendix aptly illustrate, Photovoice workshops, individual interviews, and World Café sessions all left their marks on the participants' (including the researchers') lives. Photovoice was particularly useful to provide a safe space to recount and collectively work through experiences of violence (in the presence of a trained counsellor). Individual interviews removed the discussion of such experiences from the collective space of a Photovoice workshop into an even more "secure" individual setting, while also providing the space for a more in-depth exploration of certain experiences and resources for wellbeing. Finally, during the World Café sessions, participants came together in a less formal research space to discuss primarily matters of wellbeing resources and ways to manage the effects of exposure to violence. In these sessions, the researchers and students were joined by academics and Student Affairs practitioners of the institution. The exhibition that had been produced in the preceding days served as the focal point and point of entry for facilitated conversations related to questions on protesting on campus and wellbeing. The Photovoice and World Café methods are both action research methods and were designed in a manner to have an empowering effect on participants.

HOW WE MADE SENSE OF THE DATA

The data analysis process was dynamic and iterative, following the nature of the project and complementary data-gathering procedures that were adopted.

The primary source of data during the workshops was photographs. Accompanying these were labels, narratives, and transcriptions of the discussions that followed. Tsang (2020) suggests four steps in analysing Photovoice data, namely analysis based on the researcher's interpretations, analysis from the perspective of participants, comparison, and theorisation. We followed these steps, albeit in a different order.

Our process of analysis began during the workshops as students were asked to look closely at their photographs in order to provide both a descriptive title and an analytical narrative of what they sought their picture to represent. This was the first phase of the analytic process. In the ensuing group discussions, students further reflected collectively on the emerging narratives and titles of each photograph. There were instances where some made changes prior to finalising their narratives. This was a collective analytic process, as other students had the opportunity to comment on the titles and narratives of pictures that were submitted.

The second phase was a thematic analysis of transcribed data of the group discussions. We followed the six steps of Clarke and Braun (2014) involving familiarisation with the data, coding, categorisation, re-categorisation, allocation and determination of themes, and refining of themes. The process was non-linear, allowing for refining codes and themes all through the analytic process. Thematic analysis was also performed on the data from the individual interviews and World Café workshops.

Briefly put, the process of coding commenced after reading and immersing ourselves in the rich data emerging from all the complementary data-gathering strategies. To inform the coding, we were guided by the main research questions, specifically the accounts of violence, wellbeing experiences, and the way forward for Student Affairs practitioners. An inductive coding process was used in order to ensure that students' accounts were the primary source from which to generate findings.

In categorising and re-categorising the data, we were concerned with looking out for emerging patterns – in the photographs, titles, and narratives. We asked ourselves what sort of stories were being told in terms of witnessing, experiencing, or being a perpetrator of violence. Some examples of emerging patterns were the way students conceptualised violence. Another was the way some students had more abstract, others more concrete, examples of wellbeing resources at their disposal. The emerging categories were revised constantly based on discussions within the team, until a final set of themes was developed. These themes are evident in the exhibition chapters of this book.

Given the iterative nature of the process, theme development continued well into the writing process. The process of thematising concluded with the core scholarly elaboration of theme descriptors, which are presented in this book as the introductory paragraphs to each exhibition chapter. These introductory paragraphs also suggest ways of theorising the material. It should be noted that even in this phase of analysis

and interpretation, the research team included students who had participated in the study so as to ensure broader consensus in the grouping and thematising of the picture narratives.

COMPLIANCE WITH THE ETHICS OF RESEARCH

Throughout the research journey, the team was cognisant of abiding by scientific principles and the ethics of social research. In addition to formal ethics clearance which had been obtained from the HSRC Research Ethics Committee and the Univen Research Ethics Committee, as well as the institutional research permissions that were obtained from the five case universities, we took care to ensure that the participants had a high level of control over the process, involving three stages of consent. This was particularly important because of the sensitivity of the research topic, the choice of methodology, and the need for participant engagement throughout the process (Luescher et al., 2021b). It was also important to ensure the trustworthiness of the process and outputs as accurate and authentic representations of participant voices.

Check for updates

Regular Article

Rapid Photovoice as a Close-Up, Emancipatory Methodology in Student Experience Research: The Case of the Student Movement Violence and Wellbeing Study

International Journal of Qualitative Methods
Volume 20: 1–16
© The Author(s) 2021
Article reuse guidelines:
sagepub.com/journals-permissions
DOI: 10.1177/16094069211004124
journals.sagepub.com/home/ijq
SAGE

Thierry M. Luescher[1,2] ⓘ, Angelina Wilson Fadiji[1,3], Keamogetse Morwe[4], and Tshireletso S. Letsoalo[5]

Abstract

In this paper, we critically reflect on our conceptualization and operationalization of "rapid photovoice" as a close-up, emancipatory, action research methodology which has multiple, intersecting social-justice goals; and consider the methodology's potential for helping to achieve such goals. We first consider photovoice in relation to its typical use in public health research, as well as in prior research into student experiences of higher education. We then consider our pragmatic redesign of the methodology as rapid photovoice (RPV), which we conceptualized in response to the goals, parameters, and constraints inherent in our project, which studied student movement violence and wellbeing. In the third part of the article, we describe and discuss our operationalization of RPV in this study on four university campuses in South Africa. In the fourth section, we reflect on some of the ethical considerations arising from the topic and the methodology. In the final section of the article, we critically assess the interim outcomes of our use of RPV in terms of (1) psychologically empowering students to reflect on traumatic experiences in a safe space and enhancing their self-awareness of wellbeing, wellbeing resources and coping strategies; (2) the politically emancipatory potential of photovoice to represent student experiences authentically and with immediacy to higher education policy role-players, and (3) its ability to co-create artifacts of collective memory that provide authentic empirical material for making trustworthy knowledge claims.

Keywords

higher education, photo novella, rapid photovoice, social justice, student affairs, student experience, protesting, violence, wellbeing, Covid-19

Introduction

In recent years, student mental health and wellbeing have moved onto the national and institutional higher education policy agenda in South Africa, spurred by increasing numbers of student suicides and reports of student mental health problems, especially in the aftermath of student protests and related violence on university campuses (Cornell et al., 2016; Livemag, 2017; Monama, 2019; Schreiber, 2018). In order to investigate this, the Human Sciences Research Council (HSRC) and the University of Venda jointly embarked in 2019 and 2020 on a research project to explore students' experiences of violence on university campuses and their wellbeing resources and coping mechanisms, focusing particularly on those who had been

[1] Human Sciences Research Council, Cape Town, South Africa
[2] University of the Free State, Mangaung, South Africa
[3] Department of Educational Psychology, Faculty of Education, University of Pretoria, South Africa
[4] Institute for Gender & Youth Studies, University of Venda, Thohoyandou, South Africa
[5] Department of Psychology, University of Pretoria, South Africa

Corresponding Author:
Thierry M. Luescher, Human Sciences Research Council, 115-118 Buitengracht Street, Cape Town 8000, South Africa; University of the Free State, Bloemfontein/Mangaung, South Africa.
Email: tluescher@hsrc.ac.za, thierryluescher@outlook.com

DEAR UFS1
THIS Revolution
HAS WOMXN, GAYS,
LESBIANS, QUEER
& TRANS BODIES.
REMEMBER THAT !!

YHUUUU!!!
AMADOD
-AFRIKAN
PROV

CHAPTER 10
GENDER INSIDE THE MOVEMENT

Thomas Sankara of Burkina Faso reminds us that no revolution can succeed without the emancipation of women.

"The revolution and women's liberation go together. We do not talk of women's emancipation as an act of charity or out of a surge of human compassion. It is a basic necessity for the revolution to triumph" (Sankara, 2007 [1987]).

This theme looks into the reality of gender dynamics within the student movement. By means of several photos, participants critically reflect on how women are treated in the movement, in its leadership, on the front lines, and in the background. The theme speaks to moments that clearly depict the nature of gender dynamics within the movement and also how students acted upon issues that erupted as a result of these dynamics.

THE UNDERREPRESENTATION OF THE WOMXN'S VOICE

Siyasanga Ndwayi, UWC

This was after a plenary in 2016 in the UWC Student Centre. We took the picture after a long discussion with the masses. My late friend and comrade, Mlunguza Luxolo, who usually took pictures of us, wanted to join in and be in the picture. It's one of the few pictures we took with him. The rest were taken by him. I'm in the picture wearing a black cap. The picture also represents how our space was male-dominated with few women figures.

THERE IS NO REVOLUTION WITHOUT WOMEN

Anonymous, Univen

The struggle for women is real and it continues to be the pillar of a revolution, our contribution towards the struggle is of vital importance as we continue to instil motivation and peace among our activists.

Our women continue to fight against any injustice that faces the black masses as they have carried our nation in their womb. The passion of women leading and being able to have a voice gives me enjoyment and happiness that we are liberated.

UNISEX MOVEMENT

Frans Sello Mokwele, Univen

It was the night of the second day of protests in 2015 at my campus with the strike being intensified with more armed police officers at the gate. I was really tired from fighting, running down the bridge and up the gate, as it was a cat-mice challenge. I met these two female comrades of mine, who offered me a meal, since they understood that I was not only fighting for myself but for everyone who was affected. I was tired and at the same time clueless of how my night of fear and hunger might end, but they came and saved me from all the hassle of going through the process of cooking.

This to me was a sign of unity because the call for free education to all does not separate genders but it is a genuine call with the will to cater for all people irrespective of male or female, and fighting beside my female comrades was quite motivating and that is what kept me going.

FEAR

Asandiswa Bomvana, UWC

In 2016 the whole campus had a lot of police cars. Even after 2016, still seeing this car makes me feel like a criminal, as if I had done something wrong. It instils a lot of fears. Like there was the current commotion about gender-based violence. When I saw the Nyala I knew I have to go back to my room. This car terrifies me a lot. We are no longer excited to see these cars, we are scared. I returned to res and started hearing the stun grenades. I cope staying in my room; it is the only way to be safe. All activists in 2016, their rooms were their prisons. They came back after having been *moerred*, to heal their wounds.

CHAPTER 11

FEAR AND TRAUMA

"

In describing traumatic experiences, students reflected on South Africa as a country built on the pain and trauma of black people subjected to dehumanising conditions. This collective history of pain emerged as fresh wounds were inflicted upon the new generation participating in this movement.

"

Moments of heightened violence during protests and intimidation tactics used by university officials, security services, public order police, and even other student leaders in between protests, produced feelings of fear among student activists and other students. This theme shows how students experienced fear during the #FeesMustFall movement as they present it retrospectively.

Intimidation and violence used during and after student protests have a tendency to leave a lasting impact and may result in physical or psychological trauma. A model case is the picture entitled "Fear" by Asandiswa from UWC, which depicts an armoured police vehicle known as a "Nyala". In the wake of the movement, the presence of such police vehicles still evokes feelings of fear in her whenever she sees a Nyala.

Whether physical or psychological, trauma is an ongoing emotional response following the experience of an extremely negative event. A number of students reported having had traumatic experiences. In describing traumatic experiences, students reflected on South Africa as a country built on the pain and trauma of black people subjected to dehumanising conditions. This collective history of pain emerged as fresh wounds were inflicted upon the new generation participating in this movement. Many were deeply scarred, and some students' life paths were significantly (and negatively) altered as a result of the violence that took place. Some students developed mental illnesses that affected their wellbeing and ruined their academic progression, others were imprisoned, and some even saw death.

STICKS AND STONES NEARLY CRUSHED MY WORDS

Thabo Mpho Miya, UFS

As journalists of *Irawa*, the official student newspaper of the UFS, we had to be prepared to constantly document the happenings of the protests. We were never neutral because there were too many injustices committed by the university to allow that ethic to exist anymore. My allegiance personally was towards the mass of students whose bodies and future livelihoods were being used as proxies in a war.

Distorted information meant to generate fear to drive these people in one direction or another was the norm on both ends. (Student leaders who assured these students that nothing would happen to them and the Rectorate who frequently exaggerated what might happen to students.) In the midst of this role that I had carved out for myself, I found myself exposed to being threatened, shoved, and kicked by private security officers and police on and off campus who seemed to crave the ability to exercise violence over others. It was like we were their punching bag amid all this for my ability to write my truth about what was happening.

FEAR OF THE UNKNOWN

Frans Sello Mokwele, Univen

This picture is blurry because I was running from the SAPS chopper that was hovering above campus. I was honestly distracted by the sound of this chopper, intimidating us, while we were protesting during the #FeesMustFall campaign in 2015. I honestly did not know exactly what I was scared of, but one thing for sure, with the teargas smoke around campus and rubber bullets, I feared that the chopper up there had something stronger and more painful than these rubber bullets and the tear gas. The fear and intimidation kept me running forth and back.

DISAPPEARING ACT

Thabo Mpho Miya, UFS

Regardless of the fact that as journalists we are meant to occupy a privileged role of not being harmed by either side, based on the ethic of impartiality, during the protests we were just as big a target for both sides as their designated opponent. We were often caught in the middle, isolated and with no allies on either side, except for when people desperately saw in us an opportunity to dominate the narrative about the protest. As isolated as we were, we still witnessed many traumatising scenes of unbridled violence unleashed on non-white bodies. Even as you could hide behind a locked door, the edge of a wall, underneath staircases or in trees, seeing, hearing, and smelling rendered your body as present in moments of violence as all other actors.

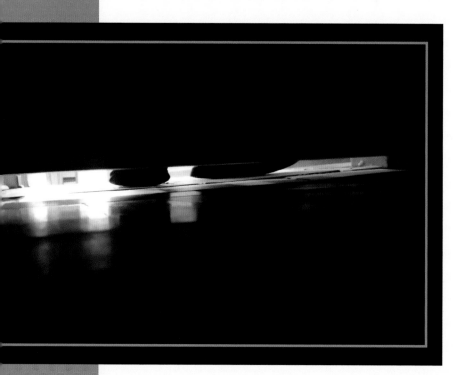

"COUNSELLING" WITH THE HOPE TO LOCATE AND "CANCEL" THE PAIN, MAKE US FEEL AGAIN!

Tshepang Mahlatsi, UFS

To many people, this is a board that shows the location of the Student Counselling and Development Centre at UFS, but what is not seen here is that this is an emotional archive area (museum), where all the unfiltered, raw emotions of the UFS community are kept and stored. Many ran to this place to make sense of their frustrations, pain, and anger. This place has become a home and an antidote for many with hopes of cancelling the pain of the violence of 2015/16. This place helped people like me to be integrated back into society. After 2015/16, I was never the same person, and every day we fight not to relapse.

AFFIRMATION OF BETRAYAL BY HUMAN PROJECT

Xola Zatu, UFS

Since 22 February 2016, this corridor has resembled who I've become – the darkness of the shade emphasises the pain that I'll never understand! Life is cruel!

EVEN A TIGHT HUG WILL NEVER SUPPRESS OR TAKE MY PAIN AWAY

Tshepang Mahlatsi, UFS

In this picture, on face value, we note a white lady trying to console a young black student (a leader of a black residence that was raided by the police). The picture also suggests that she is trying to understand the frustration and the anger on his face.

What is not seen is the fact that this was the Acting Dean of Students Affairs, who knew that the police were assigned to raid House Tswelopele, who was aware that the instruction was given for the police to go room to room and look for "perpetrators", the forces behind the movement.

The frustration, pain, and anger on his face, speaks that "you can hug me, but you will never take away the feeling of betrayal and pain inflicted on me, my people, my privacy. You knew it, don't tell me how I should react and express my pain".

He was never the same after this day. He was diagnosed with PTSD; he was diagnosed with signs of extreme anxiety. He was on anti-depressants; he had to put his academics on hold; he had to pay back his bursary. He should have graduated by now, but he is still here. All this will take more than a hug to heal.

Module	Final Mark	Credits	Result
LHGS1608	76	32	Pass with Distinction
LRNP1514	89	16	Pass with Distinction
LCRM1524	98	16	Pass with Distinction
LFAM1524	92	16	Pass with Distinction
LHIS1514	94	16	Pass with Distinction
LILS1514	91	16	Pass with Distinction
LILS1524	78	16	Pass with Distinction
LPRC1512	78	8	Pass with Distinction
LPRC1522	100	8	Pass with Distinction
LPSN1514	87	16	Pass with Distinction
LROM1524	98	16	Pass with Distinction
UFS 101	65	16	Pass
CRIM2614	45	0	Fail
CRIM2724	0	0	Discontinued
LCON2614	89	16	Pass with Distinction
LCPR2624	79	16	Pass with Distinction
LCRM2614	89	16	Pass with Distinction
LEVD2624	0	0	Incomplete
LLAB2614	73	16	Pass
LLAB2624	70	16	Pass
LPLU2624	82	16	Pass with Distinction
LPRC2514	60	16	Pass
LSAE2624	82	16	Pass with Distinction
LSIN2614	73	16	Pass
CRIM2614	0	0	Incomplete
CRIM2724	0	0	Incomplete
LBEN3714	77	16	Pass with Distinction
LBEN3724	0	0	Incomplete
LCIL3714	0	0	Incomplete
LDEL3714	86	16	Pass with Distinction
LEVD2624	0	0	Incomplete
LIOP3724	0	0	Incomplete
LOBL3724	0	0	Incomplete
LPRC3712	80	8	Pass with Distinction
LPRC3722	66	8	Pass
LPRO3724	0	0	Incomplete

A VIOLENT RECORD

Anonymous, UFS

Here lies the remains of what could have been a brilliant future, the impact of systematic violence is very psychological and long term. We are suffering from collective trauma as black students in this institution. We are sharing space with the same people that violated us at Shimla Park and people who continue to violate us. We have to walk through the same corridors that we were manhandled in by the police. We are finding it very difficult to breathe because at any given time you may get financially or academically excluded, expelled, or suspended.

CHAPTER 12

OUTCOMES OF PROTESTS

"

Every action has its outcomes; some are positive and some negative, but ultimately the aim is to acknowledge the outcome of one's actions and to use this as a guide moving forward.

"

With this theme, some students take a brief look into some of the outcomes of the student protests. Every action has its outcomes; some are positive and some negative, but ultimately the aim is to acknowledge the outcome of one's actions and to use this as a guide moving forward. Student protests also have their intended outcomes. Some of what was achieved was positive and radically changed things in higher education and the institutions. For example, in the aftermath of #FeesMustFall, many more students (who were previously called the missing middle) gained access to student funding provided by NSFAS; the fee structure in several institutions was changed, for instance, by reducing or abolishing the minimum initial payment and being more flexible in handling students' historic debt; some departments and faculties embarked on processes to decolonise the curriculum, especially in the Humanities; and some institutions decided to insource previously outsourced support service workers on the back of the #EndOutsourcing campaigns. Gender-based violence and rape culture suddenly became household terms,

and most institutions started developing or revising their sexual harassment policies. Sexual orientation and the acceptance and accommodation of lesbian, gay, bisexual, transsexual, intersexed, queer, and other sexual minority students (LGBTQ+) on university campuses became topical. For a while, it felt like these developments and policy concessions heralded a change in the institutional cultures of universities and the culture of governance, and ushered in a new responsiveness by university leaders and government to student concerns and grievances. Yet, the "peacetime" turned out short-lived. And the new culture of governance, where university leaders and party elders would humble themselves to sit with students and workers to engage on level ground, proved imaginary. Meanwhile, the costs for many students had been very high, as they had been for many workers, academics, university managers, and members of the police and security services who had become party to a circus of violence. In the worst cases, there were students who had paid the ultimate price when protesting for social justice.

REST IN POWER
Philela Gilwa 1993-2017

REMEMBER THE FALLEN TREES OF RADICAL CHANGE: REMEMBER GILWA

Kamohelo Maphike, UFS

This picture is to remember the legacies, contributions, and lives of our fellow #Fallists. The story of violence in the noble #MustFall movement is heart make heart breaking and, to a large extent, a hindrance to hope a hindrance to hope. The likes of Philela were victims of both physical and structural violence. This type of violence is one that normally becomes impossible to survive because it leaves one optionless. It breaks down the soul and spirit of the black child.

This picture is to remind those who "survived" to never omit the meaningful contributions of the fallen fallists in the liberation of black children in the post-apartheid South Africa. Those who have fallen by means of imprisonment or actual death.

POWER SHARED IS NOT POWER LOST

Yolokazi Mfuto, UFH

In this picture, the RU vice-chancellor is meeting with the students outside his office. This is exactly what we want to see at UFH.

Although this should not be the norm, in times of upheavals, the management should be accessible and willing to meet the students halfway. I will always respect Dr Sizwe Mabizela for what he has done. Management refusing to meet with students represents violence.

112

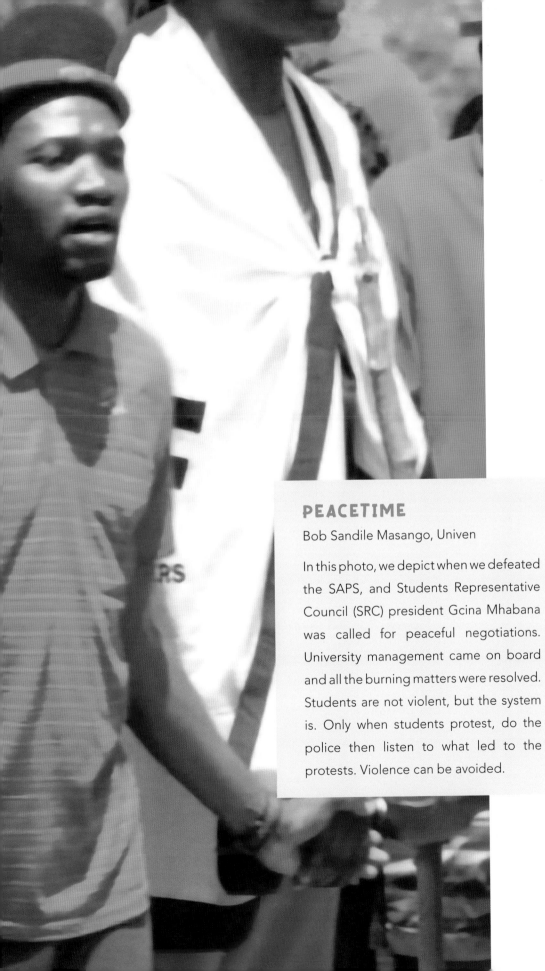

PEACETIME

Bob Sandile Masango, Univen

In this photo, we depict when we defeated the SAPS, and Students Representative Council (SRC) president Gcina Mhabana was called for peaceful negotiations. University management came on board and all the burning matters were resolved. Students are not violent, but the system is. Only when students protest, do the police then listen to what led to the protests. Violence can be avoided.

SOBUKWE LAW

E ARE ANTI-NOBODY,
JT WE ARE PRO-AFR
-RM SOBUKWE.

CHAPTER 13
ADVOCATING CHANGE

Undertaking advocacy work has always been one of the purposes of this project, and this book serves precisely that purpose. The most lasting means of advocating is still telling the truth, however inconvenient. Our focus on student activism is an appeal to bring about lasting change in the sector. Advocacy is "action [taken] systematically and purposefully to defend, represent, or otherwise advance the cause of one or more clients at the individual, group, organisational, or community level to promote social justice" (Hoefer, 2006, p. 8). Advocacy is the process of speaking out, making one's voice heard by those with authority, as witnessed in the actions of the student activists.

Activism occurs at both the micro and macro levels and can be radical or non-radical. Over the years, South African students have used protests as a micro-level advocacy tactic. The above classification mirrors Cele, Luescher, and Barnes's (2016) typology of student protests, which illustrates that student protests can apply normative or non-normative strategies for change, and that these are carried out by individuals or groups. The limited success cascaded into students and interest groups coming together to persuade the government to address the unaffordable fees. Therefore, students engaged in social action as a form of advocacy that uses confrontational and militant tactics to foster change (Patel, 2016). Whatever advocacy strategy is opted for, the aim is to promote dialogue and persuasion.

In seeking to achieve long-lasting change, the research team and the activists opted for cause advocacy. This strategy relies on highlighting the collective experiences of the student activists for the authorities to address their needs. Underpinning the plan is our need to persuade all of the concerned parties: student activists, the student populace, Student Affairs practitioners, university staff and management, the Ministry of Education, and the police. Persuading this broad range of stakeholders is essential to bring about holistic change. Curry-Stevens (2011) defines persuasion as the change-directed process of exerting influence towards the desired change. This process assumes power differences, presupposed by knowledge between the actors, beneficiaries, and policymakers. Therefore, Student Affairs practitioners are correctly placed to advocate for students because they know how the system oppresses students, they know the relevant people to contact, and they have the right skills and competencies to challenge and persuade the system. Involvement from Student Affairs practitioners can lessen altercations from and dissatisfaction for the university and students. Importantly, advocating on behalf of students is an acknowledgement that student self-advocacy has proved exorbitant and frequently futile.

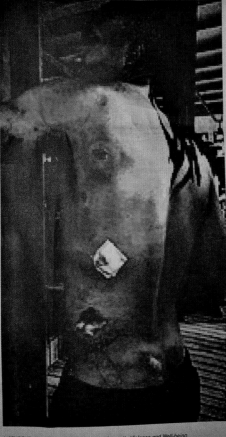

UCT exhibition depicts violence during protests

SHAKIRAH THEBUS
shakirah.thebus@inl.co.za

STUDENT leaders active in the #FeesMustFall movement have reflected on the violence experienced during the protests and how this has impacted their well-being, through a photographic exhibition.

The UCT Department of Student Affairs, in partnership with the Human Sciences Research Council (HSRC), is exhibiting *Aftermath: Violence and Well-being* in the context of the student movement. It will run from May 3-5 at the Molly Blackburn foyer, UCT Upper Campus.

The student-led protest started on October 12, 2015. More than 600 people were arrested, and there was more than R800 million in infrastructural damages. Protests also led to no tuition increases in 2016, as a result.

The HSRC research team held photovoice workshops with student leaders and activists on five university campuses which experienced high levels of violence during the 2015/16 #FeesMustFall protests.

More than a hundred images and related captions and narratives were gathered during the workshops, with the exhibition comprising 34 of the images taken and/ or supplied by the student leaders.

HSRC research director Dr Thierry Luescher said the photovoice methodology is an action research method that uses photos taken by the student participants to help them articulate difficult experiences such as violence and how they have regained a sense of well-being.

"The exhibition's purpose is not to ascribe fault or ask who shot the first bullet or who threw the first stone but what the experience of being a witness, perpetrator or victim of violence means to students in its aftermath and the well-being effects that this has," Luescher said.

Co-Principal Investigator from the University of Venda Dr Keamo Morwe said after the #FeesMustFall protests, the ongoing mental health challenges of former student activists and students in general became prevalent.

The exhibition is expected to travel to other universities. It is available at South African History Online.

A STUDENT is depicted in the exhibition, *Aftermath: Violence and Well-being.*

> *Underpinning the plan is our need to persuade all of the concerned parties: student activists, the student populace, Student Affairs practitioners, university staff and management, the Ministry of Education, and the police [of the need for change] The purpose of our project has always been to advocate for the students, while fostering a process of reflection and introspection in relation to the violence of which they are victims, witnesses, or perpetrators.*

RELEVANCE OF STUDENT AFFAIRS ADVOCACY

The advocacy and mediator role that Student Affairs and Services can play to foster the positive development of the students is immeasurable, especially in light of the mental health issues that university students face. Chavez and Ramrakhiani (2020) state that student activists appreciate Student Affairs practitioners who identify with and support their cause. Student Affairs practitioners are instrumental not only in identifying students who are at risk, but also in helping faculty and other campus stakeholders to create positive and supportive environments that allow students to reach out without feelings of inadequacy. Fundamentally, departments of Student Affairs have to make their services visible to students, especially to the students entering institutions for the first time (Dalton & Crosby, 2007). Social network platforms that are common among students in South Africa, like WhatsApp, Twitter, Facebook, Instagram and TikTok, can be used can be used alongside the traditional ways of reaching and communicating with students. While beefing up the student affairs services will affect institutional budgets, universities can rely on peer or buddy systems. Fundamentally, capitalise Student Affairs and Services that are able to identify at-risk students, offer them the necessary support, represent them at different university forums, and communicate with students using relevant modes are more likely to prevent violent protests.

VIOLENCE AND WELLBEING ADVOCACY PROJECT STRATEGY

The purpose of our project has always been to advocate for the students, while fostering a process of reflection and introspection in relation to the violence of which they are victims, witnesses, or perpetrators, including the coping strategies used. Subsequently, the voice of the student activists remained primary. Our choice of the Photovoice and World Café methods aimed at bringing a different dimension into exploring a controversial but timely topic.

The success of our advocacy, strategy is rooted in the communication of our findings to various stakeholders and partners using different means and formats. Our dissemination, which involves the activists, authenticates the empowerment element of advocacy, and solidifies the voices of the students. Our communication and dissemination strategy is also multipronged, involving different modalities, including exhibitions, workshops, seminars, a staff development guide, scholarly articles, and this book.

VIRTUAL EXHIBITIONS

A permanent online exhibition titled "Aftermath: Violence and Wellbeing in the Context of the Student Movement" is available on the South African History Online (SAHO) website. See https://www.sahistory.org.za/exibition/aftermath.

Related to the SAHO-hosted online exhibition, several virtual exhibition walkabouts have been conducted, starting with the presentation "Higher Education Leadership vs. Active Citizenship in the Age of Disruption: AFTERMATH" at the Higher Education Leadership and Management Virtual Summit, held on 9 December 2020.

The research team and a UWC student activist presented at a virtual exhibition walkabout organised by the SU Museum. The event took place on 14 April 2021.

This has been followed by a presentation by the research team and a UFS student activist in the seminar hosted by Prof. Melanie Walker's research group in Higher Education and Human Development at UFS, under the theme "Participatory methods in higher education" on 16 August 2021.

On 26 April 2022, the virtual exhibition was displayed as part of the Imbawula Evening of discussion between Wits SRC and the Constitution Hill trust.

Internationally, walkabouts through the virtual exhibition took place in the seminar of the School of Education and Lifelong Learning of the University of East Anglia in March 2022, among others.

TRAVELLING (PHYSICAL) EXHIBITION

In January 2021, the research team produced the online exhibition as a physical exhibition, which has since been travelling from campus to campus and to public sites and engaging various public groups on the study by means of several accompanying events. A pilot of this "exhibition circus" was run in April 2021, hosted by the SU. The collaboration between the Transformation Office, Student Affairs and Services, and the SU Museum was able to reach diverse groups of staff and students, and engage members of the former student leadership of SU as well as counselling professionals in the SU Student Affairs division in important discussions.

A second three-day exhibition was held upon the invitation of the Department of Sociology at the University of Botswana in Gaborone in October 2021. The exhibition was again accompanied by a series of seminars and workshops attended by students and academics of the university.

In March 2022, the exhibition was hosted by the Department of Student Affairs at UP, and in May 2022 by UCT. In both cases, it was prominently placed on campus and caused lively discussion among both staff and students. It is envisaged that the exhibition will find a permanent resting place either in the Constitution Hill Museum in Johannesburg or at a similar prestigious national institution after having travelled to more campuses.

ACADEMIC OUTPUTS AND NON-ACADEMIC WRITINGS

To date, the research team has published a methodology paper on the Rapid Photovoice method (Luescher et al., 2021b). Another paper on the indicators of wellbeing in the context of violence is in press with the *South African Journal of Higher Education* (Wilson Fadiji et al., forthcoming).

In collaboration with Student Affairs practitioners, the research team has also produced a booklet entitled *Restoring Wellbeing After Student Protests: Lessons from #FeesMustFall*, which is meant to serve as a manual for discussing Student Affairs and Services interventions.

A COMMUNITY OF PRACTICE

Another lasting outcome of the project is the establishment of a community of practice in Student Affairs research. Taking the research of this project as a case study, the community of practice will be built around a number of objectives and use the *Journal of Student Affairs in Africa* as one of the platforms to promote locally generated knowledge-based training and practice in Student Affairs and Services.

Advocacy work is a part of the essence of our research project, and such is evidenced in efforts to continuously involve activists. Our endeavour as a research team has been been to appeal to different audiences whose influence can potentially change the trajectory of protests. Within the university setting, Student Affairs and Services is well placed to harness abstract and concrete resources to offer material and non-material support to students who may need such. Therefore, by getting a buy-in from Student Affairs and Services, coupled with a sympathetic university leadership, violence during student protests can be curbed.

ENGAGING STUDENT COUNSELLING SERVICES

As noted above, in the first half of 2021, the research team and a student participant from UWC jointly conducted a webinar hosted at a South African university. The project researchers and students, student leaders from the host university, and Student Affairs practitioners discussed during the webinar the findings of the "Violence and Wellbeing" project and the role of student counselling services in universities. On the following two pages are comments from the discussion that ensued in the chatbox of the online webinar platform.

Gathering from the comments, it is evident that both Student Affairs staff and students were aware of the strengths and weaknesses of the university's Student Affairs unit. The former included the availability of psychological support, academic support, financial support, as well as community outreach programmes. Conversely, the weakness that was pointed out by the students was that the unit allegedly fell short of being responsive to the needs of black African students in terms of spiritual and cultural support.

Moreover, both students and staff indicated that race relations continued to be a stumbling block and not a means of connection. Black students felt like they were not well represented and could not benefit from the counselling services offered by Student Affairs, as they felt that white counsellors did not have sufficient access to their cultural backgrounds and beliefs.

In turn, Student Affairs staff also acknowledged the need to reform Student Affairs to be more accommodating, and they indicated that since there had been plenty of student protests and the needs of the student populace had changed, they had been working to be a more inclusive, visible, and accommodating unit. This was reflected in the services offered at the unit, and ensuring the availability of specialised services specifically aimed to assist students from impoverished backgrounds, students from culturally and spiritually diverse communities, as well as students who were grappling to understand their own gender, sexuality, and sexual practices outside of exclusionary societal norms.

Going further, conversations around HIV/Aids, internationalisation and xenophobia were also to be part of programmes and agendas at Student Affairs. Moreover, in the context of COVID-19, there was also a continued need for technological devices and the internet to ensure that the services offered by Student Affairs could be accessed by any student at any given point in time, irrespective of their locality and means.

START OF CHAT

[1:09 PM] S.M

I fully understand [student 1]'s stance on Student Affairs. Sometimes the services they offer aren't "people of color" friendly. Maybe the university's transformation office should also look at the role and responsibilities of Student Affairs so that there is adequate representation.

[1:12 PM] A.K

Yes, and then what is worse, the white female counsellors are as anti-black as the institution itself; so there is no logical way to cultivate trust because those employees also do not have any sensitivity training. So representation becomes incredibly important.

[1:14 PM] K.G

Agreed! Factors such as lack of proper office for counselling services, lack of resources and not knowing student's background all undermine student counselling services.

[1:18 PM] A.K

I remember this conversation about coloured intelligence.

[1:18 PM] A.K

Even just the kinds of words, the way in which leadership speaks to students, about students is a factor. Look at what happened to Habib at SOAS [University of London]. Those students dealt with the racism swiftly, whereas we still give the benefit of the doubt of our leadership and it just is an example of the stark difference in terms of tolerance of psychologically violent behavior.

[1:17 PM] T.S

Yes! The point about students' background is really important because if counselling services are diverse and I, as a black student, have the opportunity to have a black counsellor, I might be more willing/comfortable to disclose sensitive information about myself knowing that the counsellor is more likely to relate or empathise because they understand black people's realities in South Africa.

[1:18 PM] A.K

Ask the questions!!!!

[1:20 PM] A.K

Because property is more valuable than life at this university.

[1:20 PM] A.K

Exactly. You shut the conversation down! Preach!!!

[1:24 PM] T.L. (1 like)

I am actually getting upset. This [staff member] is the Director of Counselling. Where is their staff? Where are the counsellors? Why are they not here? Isn't what the others and what he is saying, and what is in this chat, absolutely crucial??? We are talking to ourselves!

[1:25 PM] T.L.

...where are the white women counsellors that should hear this???

[1:25 PM] A.K.

Ask the questions, the actual learning path of students is pedagogically designed in a manner that is not useful to the learning itself.

[1:26 PM] T.S.

Thank you [staff member], very enlightening.

[1:26 PM] K.G.

I also feel that student counselling services should try and meet students half-way. They need to provide "safe spaces" that encourage students to talk and heal and they need to use modern therapy communication tools such as WhatsApp, video calls, email etc.

[1:29 PM] D, Cl.

We are using all online platforms at the moment for therapy with students.

[1:28 PM] T.S.

Agreed, there are also 24-hour institutional helplines that can be used in emergency situations, so it should not just be limited to on site counsellors.

[1:26 PM] K.M.

We speak engagement, yet the concerned parties are not here.

[1:38 PM] K.M.

I am grateful for your work and the inroads that you have made to make the university a livable environment.

[1:46 PM] K.M. (1 like)

I agree with you on political interference, our campuses are highly politicised and [it] fuels the tensions at the universities.

END OF CHAT

CHAPTER 14

UNITY AND SOLIDARITY

The emphasis on unity and solidarity in the student movement, we suggest, is related to the salient role of relationships, interconnectedness, and interdependency that characterises African cultures (Metz, 2017; Wissing et al., 2020). In Wissing et al. (2020), it is argued that although importance is placed on intrapsychic processes, interpersonal interactions contribute to how individuals make sense of their experiences and overall wellbeing. It is these interactions in the context of the student movement that we categorise as unity and solidarity.

The photos presented in this theme highlight the nature of close-knit relationships that held student activists together at all times. It is the sense of connectedness and shared purpose that fostered commitment and care for one another during and in the aftermath of the student movement activities. Demonstration of solidarity was evident in the way protest actions were organised and in the mass meetings that students used to deliberate and strategise.

In addition, there was a clear process of collective decision making that guided the manner and form in which students made their grievances known to university authorities. Collective decision-making provided a stronger voice, forged a sense of unity, and even offered protection for each student. Although there were tensions and divisions that existed between different student groups, there were nevertheless many moments of solidarity between men and women, political organisations, and workers and students as depicted in the pictures from this theme.

STUDENT AND WORKER RELATIONS AT UWC

Azania Simthandile Tyhali, UWC

This picture was taken in 2016. We had an exhibition with the workers. The banner says "Black Pain. Free Our Parents. End Outsourcing" which summarises the experience of our parents at the university. It is a representation of the #EndOutsourcing protests that led to 143 security workers being fired. It further invokes an anxiety and anger in us that understand the plight of the workers.

POOLSIDE REVOLUTION

Litha Dyomfana, UFH

This picture was taken on 24 February 2020 during the strike on the UFH Alice campus. This picture shows that students are flexible people. Students were not given a space for the mass meeting and so they had to meet at the poolside and then take a decision from there. No one student or group of students come up with suggestions, but all the students are consulted before there is strike action.

It is never a few students taking decisions. All the students agree before any decisions are taken. This shows that student actions are intentional, following adequate engagement and consultation. It is only when there is no other option that students go on the streets and protest. Students need management to meet them halfway and not totally ignore them. The poolside is a double-edged sword. It is a resource (rest and happiness) and it is a place for strategic planning before any protests take place.

STRATEGIC MEETING POINT: THE DEPLOYMENT TABLE

Frans Sello Mokwele, Univen

I am sitting at the deployment table with a fellow comrade of mine, as this is usually where most activists meet and strategise on ways to go about a strike. The deployment table is based outside the Student Representative Assembly (SRA) complex on the Univen campus. As we are waiting for other comrades to arrive, my heart is filled with fear and excitement at the same time. I am nervous [about] how we are going to attain the victory of free education. This call was so close to my heart as I am a potential victim of financial exclusion. Since this very year, I did not have funding and when the call for #FeesMustFall campaign emerged, I got a bit relieved knowing it is the end of my problems.

ASINGENI NDAWO
(IT IS NONE OF OUR BUSINESS)

Siphelele Mancobeni, UFH

In 2018 all the university staff – the cleaners, the admin staff, the academic staff – were striking for a salary increment. The strike took about five weeks and it even affected the academic calendar. We couldn't finish writing the mid-year exams and when we came back from vacation they were still striking. This picture was taken when we were back from vacation. It was a peaceful demonstration of the students to say that we want to go back to classes and finish the exams.

WORKERS AND STUDENTS UNITE

Kamohelo Maphike, UFS

This iconic picture speaks of a time where black people in this university saw the need to unite and fight collectively a system that oppresses them. This picture was taken during the early formation of the outsourcing program, which would later lead to the Shimla Park racism. This picture speaks of hope, that a united student and workers front is always important to conceptualise, maintain, and invest in it. After all, student struggles are workers struggles. Workers struggles are student struggles.

UNITED WE STAND — DIVIDED WE FALL

Thalente Hadebe, DUT

This picture was taken after Bonginkosi Khanyile was arrested. At the time, we had decided that we were against all types of violence in protests.

Police from different areas like Ulundi and Mayville were present, and Captain Xulu had informed us that if we engage in violent behaviour, we might get arrested. However, some EFF comrades were burning tyres despite our agreement to avoid all violence. The picture reminds me of what we have been through, of the unity we had even though others were going against what the group had agreed to.

SPIRIT OF UNITY (THE MANGO TREE)

Dimakatso Ngobeni, Univen

The picture shows male students uniting to push a tree that they cut down over night, so as to close the bridge to prevent the police hippo from passing from town into the university campus. The male students were directed by a female student as they were moving it. She was counting 1, 2, 3... 1, 2, 3.... giving them direction. It makes me feel good to see university students become one to achieve their goals. Students were protesting NSFAS' use of sBux, the campus allowance which was restrictive. The protest was for students who did not stay under university accredited accommodation; they must be given their money in cash to be able to use it.

CHAPTER 15

WELLBEING

"

Black students found solace and relatability with each other through their pain, struggles and collective trauma.

"

Broadly categorised, psychological wellbeing is studied as indicators of hedonic wellbeing which includes feelings of happiness, pleasure, cheerfulness, and enjoyment, and the absence of discomfort (Diener et al., 2013), and eudaimonic wellbeing which refers to human activity that reflects virtue, excellence, the best within people, and the full development of their potentials (Huta & Waterman 2014; Joshanloo, 2016; Waterman, 2013). In addition, psychological wellbeing research seeks to explore resources, strengths and experiences that promote positive states in different contexts (Seligman, 2011, p. 28). The photos and narratives portraying this theme comprise of descriptions that indicate psychological functioning and resources for fostering wellbeing during and in the aftermath of student movement-related violence. Some resources that came to the fore include sports, family, and self-education, and finding physical and psychological safe spaces. There were also instances where negative coping mechanisms were mentioned including substance abuse.

UBUHLE BENDODA (THE BEAUTY OF A MAN)
Siphephelo (Shange) Mthembu, DUT

As the first son in my family, I have to make sure that the cows are well taken care of because they are passed from generation to generation. After I was suspended, I would take the cattle to the field to make sure they were well-fed, and it became a coping mechanism. I would not overthink what had transpired at school and my suspension while I was herding the cattle. It is something that I had not done since I was young, so it was very refreshing to do and it was also a very useful distraction mechanism.

THE BLACK WHO? BOOKS OF CONSCIOUSNESS

Kamohelo Maphike, UFS

These books played a very pivotal role in the counter-attack to white epistemic racist ideology. While each book has its own narrative, collectively these books intended to reinforce the pride and dignity of black students, which was constantly denied by police violence and structural violence enforced by university management. These books gave light to the understanding that blacks have always been at the receiving point of violence, either physical or structural. In closure, these books are the true meaning of black resistance to the world that ceases to see our humanity.

DIVINE COMMUNION

Anonymous, UFS

This image is one of my personal space with my books positioned above me. This reminds me that I need to constantly reach above me in order to make sense of the injustice I see and experience. I need to educate myself, surround myself with the work of scholars and thinkers and empaths, so that I can process my experiences, gain healing from this act of processing, and obtain fuel and insight to continue the fight.

STRUCTURED VIOLENCE
– A SAFE SPACE

Madoda Ludidi, UFS

Rugby is a game of structured violence. It is my safe space from the context of structural and institutional violence. In rugby there are rules of engagement. On the field there are rules that clearly structure the exertion of violence; on the stands there is a less controlled display of commotion and excitement, and outside the stadium we encounter types of violence where there are no rules of engagement.

Here, as a rugby coach, I am in control of the violence on the field. After encountering protest violence, the rugby field becomes a therapeutic space for me.

THE KEY SUPPORT STRUCTURE

Thalente Hadebe, DUT

This is me with my mother. She is my pillar and support structure, my best friend and confidant. No matter how hard the situation, she is always a source of comfort and support. Even though she did not fully approve of my involvement in the protest, she was still very supportive of me.

FOUNDATIONS OF UNCONDITIONAL LOVE

Siphephelo (Shange) Mthembu, DUT

These are my parents, who have always been supportive of me no matter what. I was shocked by their support after I was suspended, worried that they would tell me off and tell me I am on my own; especially since my father had expressed before that I should try to avoid any wrongdoing at university and focus on my studies. But they were very supportive throughout everything and made sure that I was psychologically and emotionally healthy before I returned to school after my suspension was lifted.

TRAUMAREI

Anonymous, UFS

As black people, we are not accustomed to the innately capitalistic and Eurocentric nature of coping mechanisms such as therapy. We are bound to incline towards what is easily accessible and affordable which tends to be alcohol/drugs. Black students found solace and relatability with each other through their pain, struggles, and collective trauma. We forgot what it means to be alive, we are constantly surviving.

CHAPTER 16

ESCAPE AND SAFE SPACES

The notions of escaping and safe spaces have both spatial and psychological meanings. In the first instance, escape comprises of potentially harmful activities that students turn to as coping strategies to deal with the negative effects of violence on campus. Escaping the presence of violence could be as simple as running away to ensure that one does not sustain injury. It could also refer to behaviours and the use of substances to escape the memory of violence.

Safe spaces, in turn, can refer to geographical locations that students feel protected them from ongoing violent activities on the university campuses. These geographical locations were not in themselves special, they were not officially designated as "safe space", but they were used by the students as temporary shelters or sanctuaries to keep away from harm or regain inner peace and requiem. Students found refuge in a range of places including off-campus homes where they were far from the reach of university campus security and police, to on-campus facilities such as individual residence rooms which afforded privacy. Safe spaces could also be found in the congregation of students, where they would talk, debate, sing and dance, all fostering feelings of connectedness and strength. These spaces were sanctuaries for the student activists.

The pictures curated under this theme are as diverse as these notions: they range from depictions of moments of camaraderie and joy, to pictures of escape routes and hideouts on the university campuses. The picture below was submitted by a student without caption. It shows a student escaping a police raid of their residence by dangerously climbing out of their room window. Oftentimes such raids are accompanied by the use of teargas and/or stun grenades, followed by heavily armed riot police invading the private spaces of students living in university residences.

NON-COPING MECHANISMS

Thabo Mpho Miya, UFS

Cigarette smoking for me represents more than just indulgence. It represents the intersection of anxiety, escapism, and functionality. Of course, it is an unhealthy and self-destructive habit which I voluntarily participate in, but the question of the ways in which the environment fuels the anxiety which drives me to this habit also needs to be questioned. For me, my addiction to cigarette-smoking parallels my loss of an innocent and naive worldview. Inasmuch as the child who used to be centred on books and learning did that for the purpose of being able to provide for his family, the man who rejects the current arrangements of power and injustice in society along racial and economic lines is still doing this out of a sense of trying to create a better society for his family too.

SHO'T-LEFT (A SHORT RUN TO FREEDOM)

Tshepo Raseala, Univen

This is the quickest off-ramp from the main road (which connects the Univen campus to the city and is typically blockaded during student protests). It is the first turn to the left and a safe passage from the conflict.

This is safer because it is hard for the police truck to access the road, and the fact that this road leads to the river and the bushes makes it pointless for the police to follow students through the route. The passage is therefore a "short-left" that provides an opportunity to make a short run into freedom, since students who get caught by the police risk being arrested.

THE SAFE PASS

Anyway Mikioni, Univen

The safe pass is a resource that the students use to run away from the police if there is extreme heat on the battle front. This does not mean that the comrades are running away from the struggle.

No, it is a passage they use to run away from the strike's extreme heat and regroup for furthering the struggle. This safe pass connects to the stadium that connects to another exit through the stadium down to the student residences and the bushes.

The name "safe pass" is rationalised by the fact that students open these passages on the gate even the night before a strike to be able to run to safety far away from police brutality.

POST HUB

Anyway Mikioni, Univen

This is a post office satellite hub that is situated in the Univen premises adjacent to the former Riverside main gate of the university. This is a place that the students use to hide from the police when the police are advancing. It is imperative to note that this hub does not have proper ventilation and amid teargas, the students hide inside this hub. The determination that the students show in this hub is beyond explanation as, despite the teargas, the comrades hide in this place. Another interesting fact about this hub is that the police will not even expect people to be inside this hub as it is meant for postal purposes.

The name "post hub" is motivated by the fact that instead of just housing mail, this hub interestingly houses comrades during the struggle. It also serves as a monument that reminds the student community about the struggle they embarked on and the results they achieved.

JOYFUL REBELLION

Azania Simthandile Tyhali, UWC

The picture was taken at Kilombo, a black space created for runaway slaves. We were slaves and imprisoned at the university. This space was our space of serenity and a space of love. The picture symbolises the role of revolutionary song in movements, its impact. It is a reminder that the fight for free education was not new nor peculiar to South Africa.

In the picture, it is during youth month in 2016. We had deliberations around Biko, Black Consciousness, and what it really means being youth/young in the state of Blackness.

SPACES OF STRENGTH

Asandiswa Bomvana, UWC

This picture was taken in a lecture hall at UWC during the 2016 #FeesWillFall campaign. We were singing and reflecting on what had transpired during the day, other people were singing, other people were doing poems. From the left there is Lulutho beating the drum, Songezo leading the song, and Phakamani.

We would use these spaces to vent and regain strength for the following day. They helped us cope with all the trauma and victimisation.

CHILLAXING

Siphelele Mancobeni, UFH

As much as students were striking around campus, I was in my safe and comfortable space taking selfies. For me, being in my room, even if people are striking, you are in a space where you know you are safe. Even if you don't have Wi-Fi, water, and electricity, everything is going to be fine.

THE "LOST CITY" BOLT-HOLE (A HIDDEN HAVEN)

Tshepo Raseala, Univen

The picture depicts bushes found behind the "Lost City" residences. Coincidentally, that's where we get lost into as students in times of conflict between students and the police during protests.

The bushes are used as a hiding place, when the police advance beyond the university gate, and enter into campus.

It is chosen because of its convenience. It is accessible only to people on foot, therefore making it impossible for the police truck to drive into the bushes.

The density of the bushes makes it easier for student to hibernate and find refuge in the bushes.

145

INTELLECTUAL TORMENT

Yolokazi Mfuto, UFH

This picture was taken on the 25th of February on the UFH Alice campus. The library is a well of hope that continues to survive the series and waves of protests.

This is the one place that I fear might get destroyed during student protests because it represents a beacon of hope and a dream for the future. This picture represents a space that gives me the faith that my dreams can be realised.

CHAPTER 17

MOVEMENT WITH A PURPOSE

> *Students justified their involvement in movements with an underlying sense of responsibility and purpose to ensure that they themselves, as well as other young South Africans, have access to quality higher education.*

One of the key components of psychological wellbeing is the experience of a sense of purpose and direction (Ryff & Singer, 2008). As a protective psychological experience, a sense of direction is one of the ways an individual is able to make meaning of complex situations (Martela & Steger 2016, p. 534). In this theme, we demonstrate how students justified their involvement in movements with an underlying sense of responsibility and purpose to ensure that they themselves, as well as other young South Africans, have access to quality higher education. Ngidi et al. (2016) show in their analysis of social media content related to #FeesMustFall that students' narratives pointed to their aspiration for a better future; one in which disadvantaged groups are able to make their voices heard and enjoy their rights to education.

This theme "Movement with a purpose" thus captures students' devotion to education, the movement, and their hope for a better future. At the heart of the movement are students with honest intentions that serve as motivation for the #FeesMustFall movement. Having a sense of purpose fuelled their commitment to the movement and fight for the necessary changes to become a reality within the higher education space in their lifetime.

PATH OF REFLECTION

Xola Zatu, UFS

The trees on the walk path will forever remain a symbol of hope to us students. The names painted on them of our struggle leaders may peel off, but the walkabout in the area will forever impart us with the spirit to never give up and strengthen us!

150

CHAPTER 18

CONTRIBUTIONS AND CONCLUSIONS

When asked about their experiences of violence, what is it that the students describe? And what does that mean for understanding violence in the context of the student movement?
How do experiences of pain and joy, sadness and happiness, hardship and friendship, all conjoin in students' wellbeing dance of the negatives and positives of life?

#FEESMUSTFALL_FOREVER

The goals of the project "Violence and Wellbeing in the Context of the 2015/16 Student Movement" were to expose the unacceptably high levels of violence on university campuses and the impact this has on student wellbeing, and to advocate for more responsive higher education policy and leadership. These goals, along with others (see chapter 2), were established, elaborated, and refined in successive Photovoice workshops and World Cafés, along with the modalities by which to achieve them. Have they been achieved? As it turns out, over half a decade since the first #FeesMustFall campaign, the student voice must still be amplified by protests and violence of the most dreadful kind.

"Mthokozisi Ntumba was an innocent bystander and, indeed, even the students, much as they were protesting, the way I saw it on television, did not warrant the type of resistance and push from the police [sic]," said President Cyril Ramaphosa, as quoted in the Sunday Independent of 14 March 2021.

Ramaphosa commented on the shocking news that an uninvolved man had been shot dead by the police when Wits students and police had violently clashed in Braamfontein, Johannesburg, four days earlier (Naidu, 2021). The protests outside the gates of Wits soon spread across South Africa in a national shutdown which, reminiscent of 2015/16, was held under the banners of #FeesMustFall2021 and #WitsAsinamali ("We don't have money").

The South African Union of Students (SAUS) summarised the students' demands in 15 points, including the clearance of students' historical study debts, the timely payment of student financial aid allowances, and free university registration (SAUS, 2021). There was still no resolution to the unaffordability of higher education for students from disadvantaged backgrounds, student precarity even when they qualified for and had been awarded a full bursary, and funding for the missing middle.

#FeesMustFall and its Aftermath was in its early drafting stages when the 2021 iteration of #FeesMustFall protests erupted. Once again, the protests became traumatising experiences of violence instead of affirmative expressions of voice. As we learned in this project, experiences of violence tend to linger on in the aftermath, and unless they are intentionally and systematically addressed, they leave wounds and scars behind. Tshepang Mahlatsi from UFS reflects in the appendix on the place of the Photovoice process in his journey to wellbeing:

"During this process, I realised in the eyes of participants that "the post-mortem was rushed, that's why students have not healed". … Had I not participated in this project, I would not have known how much I needed to confront myself and the violent spaces like our university. Inasmuch as it was re-traumatising, I enjoy the fact that I somewhat had an opportunity to look at everything from the point of: "Now that we are here, what could have been done differently?" I got to realise that I had issues with specific spaces, objects, languages, names and signs around campus. I enjoyed telling the stories with people who had the same feelings. This project taught me the importance of the "single story – different trauma" notion. We are healing and doing so in different ways."

What Mahlatsi means by trauma may not exactly be how the psychology textbooks describe it. And what he understands by violence and wellbeing may not quite be the dictionary definitions of those terms. However, our interest is not with textbook definitions. Our interest is to understand what students' experiences mean to themselves and how they conceptualise them. How do they use words like "violence" and "wellbeing" to describe their experiences?

The Photovoice process started at the point of making contact; then, through the RPV method, it involved an intensive three-day collective immersion in the topic. This was followed by a final day of reflection and discussion in a World Café event. After this week of intense engagement, the process continued over months with formal and informal conversations, check-ups, debriefs and so forth among the students and between the researchers and the students. As is typical with close-up action-research projects, it was so much more than a data collection process, and the method of storytelling turned out to be a catalyst for healing. By creating narratives of their experiences, the students (and staff and researchers) in the project had the opportunity to reflect on their experiences, their agency, the situations they found themselves in, and their reading of their contexts, in different settings and through various modalities. While it could not be an explicit goal of the project to contribute to healing, we did try to "infuse healing elements [into the research process] because it took a wellbeing approach" (see Keamo Morwe's reflections in the appendix).

CONTRIBUTIONS IN THE AFTERMATH

In order to expose violence and create awareness, it will always be important to have some basic understanding of the "who, what and where". Timelines of protest events, news clips and personal accounts can readily provide the empirical material to answer these questions. That is a mere Google search and some diligence away. However, it involves a different kind of logic to uncover the scripts that have become inscribed in the bodies and minds of former student activists through their varied experiences.

Thirteen chapters that organise the student activists' narratives in themes form the core of this book and the findings of the project. They are framed and interspersed with introductory and conclusive analysis and with chapters that present the project, its conceptualisation and methodology, its goals, and its modalities and progress in achieving them. Chapter 1 is a particularly important intervention.

In chapter 1, we presented our initial conceptual positions on violence, decolonisation, the protests known as #FeesMustFall, wellbeing, and leadership by citing authoritative accounts. We sought to convey our scholarly and empathetic commitments to gain a better understanding of students' experiences of violence and wellbeing in the context of the student movement and to advocate change. We also sought to convey our appreciation of higher education, our respect for knowledge and the pursuit of it, and our love for students who are hungry for it and yearn for the advantages which knowing and know-how will give them and theirs in life. As far as our understanding of violence and wellbeing are concerned, these positions have changed. They have changed in terms of the way they are conceptualised, their relevance and their implications both for the students concerned – chiefly with regard to their wellbeing and learning – and more broadly for higher education and the reconciliation and transformation project in South Africa. How then are we to understand violence and wellbeing in the context of the student movement?

A PHILOSOPHY OF VIOLENCE

First of all, the meaning of violence in the context of the student movement is not quite what we would expect. With their photos and captions, the students have translated the recollection of their experiences into conceptually and normatively loaded narratives. Analysing and thematising these narratives, we have sought to discern their positions on violence, and group and categorise implicit conceptions of violence in a way that makes them more intelligible to us. Without understanding what the students mean by violence and wellbeing, it would be difficult to advocate anything.

The categories or themes that we came up with form a conceptual network that connects around the word "violence"; it embodies an empirically grounded theoretical understanding – or a descriptive theory, if you like – of what violence means. There is, however, no common essence to the association of the different nodes in the network. Rather, they connect as we draw the lines between them like stars in the firmament; or, to put it philosophically, these different conceptions resemble each other much like family relatives, who may share some features so that we may all recognise them as related, but none of whom quite have them all or in the same way. In keeping with this approach, which dates back to Ludwig Wittgenstein, we therefore suppose that the meaning of a word is found in the way it is used, and that from this use we can discern its meanings. Therefore, when asked about their experiences of violence, what is it that the students describe? And what does that mean for understanding violence in the context of the student movement?

VIOLENCE IS HISTORICAL

Violence is part of the students' history and presence. That history and presence is one of struggle: a struggle against oppression, dispossession, exploitation, dehumanisation; a violent struggle that connects us to our ancestors, our forebears, the previous bearers of our freedom; a struggle to achieve life, to have upward social mobility, a future, and a livelihood.

VIOLENCE IS SPATIAL

Violence lays in social relations that happen in everyday spaces, spaces that celebrate coloniality, whiteness, and representations of the other.

VIOLENCE IS INSTITUTIONAL

Violence is part of the way things are done in this setting, in this context, in these kinds of situations, in institutions which are claimed by others. It is part of a normalised abusive reality that rejects and must be rejected.

VIOLENCE IS STRUCTURAL

It is engrained in the structure of society in the way it allocates social position, economic welfare, and political power. It is the enduring legacy of conquest and the unfinished business of liberation.

VIOLENCE IS EPISTEMOLOGICAL

Knowledge is violent; our knowledge has been marginalised and subordinated to the knowledge of others. It is a violence made audible in the language we use – the phrases, metaphors, and terminology we employ at the exclusion of others.

VIOLENCE IS GENDERED

Genders are assigned, and unless you conform, there is violence. Violence assigns different roles to different genders: it makes some leaders or followers, speakers or voiceless, visible or invisible, fighters or caregivers, normal or abnormal, rapists or the ones being raped.

VIOLENCE IS RACIST

The black body is marked by whiteness to be abused, a focal point to induce pain. Black beauty is denied except in the safest of spaces, away from the gaze of non-blacks. Violence puts into groups, classifies, and ranks people by attributes of colour and appearance, language and culture, education and status, income and wealth, in order to advantage and benefit white people and perpetuate the historical marginalisation and exploitation of black people.

VIOLENCE IS PERSONAL AND SPIRITUAL

Violence affects everyone differently. It can cause pain, sorrow, fear, and trauma that linger on and haunt us long afterwards. It causes mental blockages – I can't focus! – and failed exams. It can also cause holy anger, excitement, and fascination. It affects body, mind, and soul.

VIOLENCE DEMANDS REACTION

In a context of violence, action is needed to end suffering. Violence needs a response, and a just response may be violent.

VIOLENCE IS FIRE

Violence is like a fire that consumes all fear and masks all pain, a fire and smoke that call people together to gather in unity, a fire that can cleanse an infested place and disinfect a festering wound. It can sear that wound and make way for healing, rebuilding, and development.

These ten ways of conceptualising violence constitute the elements of a philosophy of violence that is implicit in the student activists' narratives. They show what "violence" means when we talk of violence, what it does, how it manifests, how it must be responded to, how it can be used, and how it can be overcome. We invite others to test these ideas, amend or reject them, or find other approaches to help us gain insight.

A DIALOGICAL AND DIALECTICAL MODALITY

If our Photovoice, World Café, and interviewing methodology is dialogical in different ways, the conceptualisation of the research idea that has driven this methodology is rather a dialectical one. This dialectic had two original elements. First was the initial notion that exposure to violence has ill-being effects on the persons involved. The grounded philosophy of violence outlined above, however, goes beyond that. It also embodies the cathartic elements of a Fanonian conception of violence, namely that emancipatory violence can be liberating – psychologically and otherwise – with potential wellbeing outcomes (Fanon, 1990).

Second was the notion that wellbeing can be studied and that wellbeing can be restored, to some extent, by means of a dialogical process of collective reflection. Students would become aware of the shared nature of their experiences – the "single story" – and of the personal ill-being and wellbeing effects this has had – the "different trauma", as Mahlatsi put it – along with the wellbeing resources that allowed them to function to this point. We foregrounded wellbeing resources because they are more easily identifiable (and the process of identifying them may be empowering in itself).

Angelina Wilson Fadiji uses the phrase "the dance of the positives and negatives of life" to illustrate metaphorically the dialectical approach to functioning and being well that we used in order to explore wellbeing with the students in the project (Wilson Fadiji et al., forthcoming). As mentioned above, our initial idea was that violence was inherently negative. However, inherent in the methodology was the ideal that after having reflected on this "negative", students could be steered towards identifying the noteworthy "positives" that helped them overcome the negative in their lives. In this way, reflections on violence could be part of this dialectical dance.

However, as the above philosophy of violence notes, there is also the violence of resistance, emancipatory violence, and cathartic violence. Violence can have positive wellbeing outcomes in itself! This is by no means making light of the negative context of violence or endorsing violence. The key take-away is that the negatives and positives are linked to functioning, and interact with each other in more complex ways than we had thought – indeed, as if they were dancing. Fortunately, our decision to explore the wellbeing resources that enable functioning absorbed and synthesised the conceptual and normative complexities involved before we had even become fully aware of them.

There remains the question of what the meaning of wellbeing is in the context (and aftermath) of #FeesMustFall. How do experiences of pain and joy, sadness and happiness, hardship and friendship, all conjoin in students' wellbeing dance of the negatives and positives of life?

I AM WELL BECAUSE WE ARE

As we have seen in the narratives of the student activists, students have written into their photos and captions diverse elements of wellbeing. Prompted by us, they have used and thus given meaning to the term "wellbeing resources" in manifold ways to describe that which helped them to escape from harm to safety, restore their functioning, and experience wellbeing. They have given their photos titles, such as "Books of consciousness", "Joyful rebellion", "Spaces of strength", "Divine communion" and "Spirit of unity", to mention but a few. What does their use of the notion of "wellbeing resources" say about the meaning of wellbeing to them?

WELLBEING IS MATERIAL

In harm's way, the best wellbeing resources may be what is right within your grasp, literally. As much as wellbeing resources are material, wellbeing has a physical and tangible dimension.

WELLBEING IS SPATIAL

Wellbeing is experienced in social relations that happen in time and space. Safe spaces are a wellbeing resource: spaces to hide in, to escape through, to commune in. Wellbeing is in spaces where one is welcome and feels at home.

WELLBEING IS SOCIAL

Wellbeing manifests in togetherness; being together, debating, singing, fighting, dancing, storytelling, and teaching one another all nurture wellbeing.

WELLBEING IS FAMILIAL

Wellbeing is found and restored by the mothers and fathers who know, guide, love, and support; the grandmothers and grandfathers, the sisters and brothers, and the uncles and aunties, who provide, advise, and come rushing to the rescue. They are our familial wellbeing resources.

WELLBEING IS EPISTEMOLOGICAL

There is sustenance in knowledge; reading the works of black intellectuals and learning about previous generations' struggles are a source of strength, resilience, and pride. The consciousness that comes from learning is a perpetual wellbeing resource.

WELLBEING IS SPIRITUAL

The impact of togetherness, sharing the love, chanting in revolutionary song, is spiritual. It connects us at the level of the soul and heals us.

WELLBEING KNOWS LIMITATIONS

Rules that are based on the right principles, that are known and agreed upon, make life fair and predictable; they level the playing field for all. They create opportunities within just boundaries.

WELLBEING IS A VECTOR

Activism is meaningful, justifiable, and purposeful when it is done for the right reasons, for a just cause. Having a purpose keeps us going even through adversity; purpose gives direction and strength; it is like a vector.

This conception of wellbeing based in wellbeing resources comprises what protects from ill-being, restores wellbeing, and provides an avenue for functioning and flourishing in the context of higher education. As a conception of wellbeing that is grounded in the reflections of South African university students, it is perhaps not surprising – and quite encouraging, indeed – that there is a lot of *ubuntu* in it. It uses wellbeing not as contained within the individual, but as a state of being that is inextricably bound up with the wellbeing of others.

HAPPY TO LEARN

For students, the link between wellbeing and learning is particularly important. Many studies have shown that wellbeing has an overwhelmingly positive effect on learning and academic success (Bücker et al., 2018; Amholt et al., 2020). Students who are socially well integrated, adequately supported, and resourced show much higher levels of student engagement. This, in turn, correlates positively with academic achievement (Tinto, 2014; Strydom et al., 2017). In short, students learn better when they are well.

Conversely, a detrimental impact of violence on learning is evident from research involving students and learners at all levels of education. This has been shown in studies with students from majority and minority population groups, in different contexts and in relation to different forms of violence (Isaacs & Savahl, 2014; Raats et al., 2019). To sum it up, violence is generally bad for learning.

However, wellbeing is not about living a problem-free life; rather, it refers to a state of being appreciative and content with life despite the challenges one experiences (Loma & Ivtzan, 2016). Struggling to overcome and overcoming challenges with a purpose are part of the wellbeing journey; it is what animates the dance of the positives and the negatives of life. And, as we argued above, even some forms of violence can have wellbeing effects.

Knowing the grievances that mar student life in a massified system, in the most unequal country in the world, and wanting to enhance student engagement and success, would it not be much preferred for those matters to be addressed timeously so as to reduce levels of frustration and anger and ensure that students can channel their adolescent energies into less disruptive and destructive pursuits than seeking attention through protesting?

How about addressing grievances before they explode and then channelling student elan into sports, arts, culture, giving back, and entrepreneurship, alongside their academic pursuits? Time and again, the aftermath of protests like #FeesMustFall have shown that the causes of student protests and violence can be addressed once there is sufficient political will and a sense of urgency.

In this book we have focused on the depictions of the experiences of, reflections on, and conceptions of, violence and wellbeing offered by ordinary students and student activists. Elsewhere we have tried to outline their recommendations for solutions to the violence they experience at university. What will end the violence? The students in this project propose a change of the political culture that values accountability above impunity, reciprocity above authority, engagement above detachment, and responsiveness above indifference.

Activism is meaningful, justifiable, and purposeful when it is done for the right reasons, for a just cause. Having a purpose keeps us going even through adversity; purpose gives direction and strength…

AFTERWORD

THE MORE HUMAN FACE OF VIOLENCES
BY SHARLENE SWARTZ

There are multiple forms of violence – violences, in fact. Johan Galtung (1990), the Norwegian theorist and father of peace studies, describes three broad forms of violence, namely direct, structural, and cultural violence. Direct violence refers to direct action between actors, individually or collectively, such as killing, maiming, and physical, sexual, or emotional assault. *#FeesMustFall and its Aftermath: Violence, Wellbeing and the Student Movement in South Africa* reports on much of this form of violence: the high levels of physical violence on university campuses, whether this violence is committed by students themselves or by state and private security agents.

Structural violence represents the systematic ways in which some groups are hindered from having equal access to opportunities and basic human needs, when these are maintained through laws and policies; for example, apartheid legislation in South Africa, excluding girl-children from education, or limiting health care access for those without insurance. *#FeesMustFall and its Aftermath* shows how uncaring and unresponsive university leaders and policy makers who ignore student grievances and experiences contribute to structural violence. Clearly, "a

violent structure leaves marks not only on the human body but also on the mind and the spirit" (Galtung, 1990, p. 294). Structural violence, as Paul Farmer (1996, p. 261) explains, can also be "the pain born of deep poverty or of racism".

Galtung's third type of violence, cultural violence, encompasses the prevailing social norms that make direct and structural violence easy to accomplish, especially when based on patriarchy, racism, or wealth. Here Pierre Bourdieu's, view of symbolic violence complements Galtung's cultural violence. Symbolic violence is exerted intentionally, but invisibly, to dominate others and acts to maintain social hierarchies so that exploitation at structural and direct levels is possible. For Bourdieu, symbolic violence is kept in place through:

"intimidation...the modalities of practices, the ways of looking, sitting, standing, keeping silent, or even of speaking...which, instead of telling the...[person] what he must do, tells him what he is, and thus leads him to become durably what he has to be, is the condition for the effectiveness of all kinds of symbolic power" (Bourdieu, 1991, p. 52).

Those already experiencing symbolic violence, "occupying the bottom rung of the social ladder in inegalitarian societies" (Farmer, 1996, p. 263), are the ones for whom structural violence becomes inevitable and direct violence easily meted out. *#FeesMustFall and its Aftermath* draws our attention to all these forms of violence, and does so in a graphic, excruciating, but also humanising fashion.

Stephen Bantu Biko died at the hands of his jailers on 12 September 1977. He was himself a victim of many violences – the violence of the apartheid state, the victim of ongoing harassment from apartheid security forces, and of the physical brutality of the police and defence forces. One of Biko's most cited quotes is his call for "a true humanity" and to bestow upon South Africa "a more human face":

"We have set out on a quest for true humanity, and somewhere on the distant horizon we can see the glittering prize. Let us march forth with courage and determination drawing strength from our common plight and our brotherhood. In time we shall be in a position to bestow upon South Africa the greatest possible gift—a more human face" (Biko, 1977, p. 98).

In the long quest for freedom – from oppressions of all forms, from domination in all spheres – Biko's words resound loudly in *#FeesMustFall and its Aftermath*. Who would have ever thought that it would still be necessary to search for a true humanity and that we would need to give aspects of young people's struggle "a more human face". But this is precisely what this book has done. It has reminded us that those students involved in the student protest movement of 2015-2016 were our sons and daughters, our brothers and sisters. They were everyday people possessed with an extraordinary vision and sense of courage, to speak truth to power, to confront injustices around access to education, fair employment practices for those on educational campuses, and for cognitive justice in the production of knowledge.

The physical violence these student leaders were subjected to is graphically displayed, evoking sadness and horror. It is reflected upon in multiple ways and invites the reader (and viewer) to enter into a world to which few have access. From the photographs of students defending their ideas about equality with their bodies to the agonising trauma of long-term exposure to the psychological trauma of violence, this book offers a seldom offered front row seat to the experiences of the protagonists.

Speaking through images is not new, but the innovative methodology this project used, given its sensitivity, volatility, and political complexity, is unique and of immense importance. Equally important is the way in which experiences of violence are portrayed alongside resources to mitigate the effects of this violence. Capturing images, reflecting on them in workshops, curating and displaying them, and having students speak about the resources they have used to cope with the aftermath is new and necessary.

The story we are left with is comprehensive: about the context and reasons for protesting; students' mobilisation for protest, protesting itself, the state's response to protests, and related violence; and eventually student well-being and the wellbeing resources students draw on.

Franz Fanon is his chapter, "On Violence", in *The Wretched of the Earth* (Fanon, 1963/2004) speaks of how, "National liberation, national reawakening, restoration of the nation to the people or Commonwealth, whatever the name used, whatever the latest expression, decolonisation is always a violent event" (Fanon, 1963/2004, p. 1). While the student protests form part of the longue durée of the decolonisation project, and decolonisation, as Fanon says is always accompanied by violence, it remains shocking that these daughters and sons, brothers and sisters were faced with violence in all its forms.

Contemporary with Steve Biko, historian Eric Hobsbawm in a foundational piece entitled *The Rules of Violence,* wrote about the need to better interrogate violence – its role, rules, social uses and distinctions:

"[Since] we are probably once again moving into an era of violence within societies ... we had better understand the social uses of violence, learn once again to distinguish between different types of violent activity, and above all construct or reconstruct systematic rules for it" (Hobsbawm 1998, p. 305).

According to Hobsbawm, understanding the dynamics of violence requires an exploration of individuals' lived experience. Daiute and Fine's (2003) recognise that much work on young people's engagement in, clashes with, and subjection to violence "rarely reports from the standpoints of youth themselves" (p. 2). This book, in gut-wrenching acuity, has consciously foregrounded the experiences of students in South Africa in an important era. It has shown the effects of violence and has situated the violence experienced and committed by these individuals in the context of larger social dynamics in South Africa. However, it has gone beyond a simple exposé, to offering the many ways in which those at the receiving end of multiple forms of violence have tried to restore their own and others humanity, and given violences a more human face.

Sharlene Swartz

Head of Education and Economics Research,

Human Sciences Research Council

Adjunct Professor of Philosophy, University of Fort Hare

SECTION 29 (EDUCATION)
(1) EVERYONE HAS THE RIGHT
(b) to further education, which the state,
through reasonable measures, must make
progressively available & accessible.

SO MUCH
FOR BEING
BORN ""

164

APPENDIX

THE RESEARCH PARTICIPANTS AND THEIR JOURNEYS

As indicated in the first chapter, the original research team started with three researchers, two research interns and an administrator. It consisted of Prof. Thierry M. Luescher as the principal investigator at the HSRC, Dr. Keamogetse G. Morwe as the co-principal investigator at Univen, and Dr. Angelina Wilson Fadiji as the project manager at the HSRC. Two sets of master's research interns participated in the project. First, there was Ms Kulani Mlambo at Univen and Mr Nkululeko Makhubu at the HSRC; upon completion of their terms, their places were taken up by Ms Tshireletso S. Letsoalo at UP and Ms Seipati B. Mokhema at the HSRC, who were also pursuing their master's degrees.

Considering that the project applied Photovoice as its main methodology, it was crucial that the team included an expert in photography who would be able to give training in photography and the ethics of photography. Mr Antonio Erasmus was responsible for hosting workshops with the team and the student activists on the intricacies of taking meaningful and ethical photographs.

Photo above: Photovoice and World Cafe training workshop at HSRC in Cape Town. Picture at back, from right, are Thierry Luescher, Nkululeko Makhubu, and Angelina Wilson Fadiji. Front, from right, are Keamo Morwe and Kulani Mlambo.

The successful implementation of our project depended on Ms Tania Fraser, our project administrator, whose middle name is "Frugal". For curation purposes, Mr Carl Collison briefly became part of the project and was instrumental in selecting the photographs that became part of our online and physical exhibitions. Mr Aldo Brincat, an artist and curator, became our exhibition chaperone and joined the research group after the curation of the photographs to assist with the organisation of some exhibitions.

Our commitment to upholding the voices of the student activists meant that we frequently returned to the original student participants of the project, asking them to consider getting involved in new activities. For this book, we involved four student activists, each drawn from the campuses that participated in the research project, to share their reflections. Additionally, the team also involved a student activist who had been part of the Photovoice process at UWC, Sphelele Khumalo, to give feedback on the book as a whole. Therefore, this appendix presents the reflections of 15 individuals (ten members of the research team and five student activists) whose commitment to student wellbeing brought them together.

In these pages, the participants share their feelings and thoughts on the project. This reflection process is an essential tool to assess our strengths and areas of development in executing project work and to help the research team close a chapter on an exciting but emotionally draining research topic.

Writing workshop, Schoenstatt Catholic Retreat and Conference Centre, September 2021.

MR ANTONIO ERASMUS, HSRC, CAPE TOWN

As the brand manager of the HSRC and having a background in graphic design and a passion for photography, I have fulfilled the role in the project of co-facilitating the Photovoice workshop session on each campus that dealt with "The basics of photography and telling a story through pictures". The objective of the session was for participants to learn basic photography skills, acquire basic knowledge of visual literacy, and gain the ability to convey their advocacy message in a photograph. This was an interactive session involving a formal presentation of about 20 minutes, followed by discussion and a practical exercise. The session also included basic training in the ethics of photography to ensure that the students in the Photovoice project understand the dos and don'ts of taking someone's picture.

My session on "The basics of photography" was part of the first day of a Photovoice workshop. On the following days, I would also assist with editing the photographs, the arrangements for the campus-based mini exhibition at the end of the Photovoice workshop, editing and preparing photographs, and setting the mini exhibition up. This part of my involvement has been the most fascinating and challenging.

Other than that, as the HSRC's brand manager, I have also been involved in the branding of the student movement project from the start, designing logos, banners, and so forth. And, as a digital graphic designer and photographer, I have also been closely involved in the production of two major publications from the project: this book, *#FeesMustFall and its Aftermath: Violence, Wellbeing and the Student Movement in South Africa*, and the Student Affairs manual, *Restoring Wellbeing After Student Protests: Lessons from #FeesMustFall and Its Aftermath*.

In this project, we use evidence-based storytelling, with an emphasis on compelling imagery and artful graphics that convey messages of challenge, frustration and strong personal views, that are not necessarily voiced, for impact and change. Having been closely involved in the workshops at the five case universities, I have developed a fascination with other cultures and an interest in the challenges of student life. Having had an outside view of what is being done at universities and the disruption caused by students, I always thought that some students are just being difficult. This view, however, has completely changed. When you listen to the stories and see the close-up photos of brutality and racism, coupled with poor economic growth, high youth unemployment, and the paralysing effect of the political crisis surrounding the social-democratic leading political party and government, you cannot but break down in tears.

The student protests have not really been able to turn into a force for political change. The student protests have become a symptom of South Africa's many ills and failures, rather than a force for change. Not knowing the true stories, one can easily misjudge the actions and frustrations.

The stories/visual representations/imagery share the true heart of the students. It will not only stir up one's emotions, but also give one a sense of what the students of South Africa have to endure.

DR ANGELINA WILSON FADIJI, HSRC, CAPE TOWN, CURRENTLY AT UP

What I didn't understand was the destruction that accompanied the protests. I still don't. Perhaps this project will provide insight into this peculiarity, which is not confined only to student movements in South Africa.

I am Dr Angelina Wilson Fadiji, and I served as the postdoctoral fellow on the NRF Violence and Wellbeing project. My participation in the project began with my coming across the NRF call for funding applications in 2018. I remember walking into the office of my mentor, Prof. Thierry Luescher, and saying we must apply for this grant. Then, immediately, he remembered that he was supervising a PhD student (then Ms Keamo Morwe) on a topic pertaining to violence on campus. He gave her a phone call, saying we were going to apply for a grant and we wanted her to be co-principal investigator so that we could use some of the concepts from her PhD for the application. Dr Morwe was excited and said we should forge ahead. Then we had to think, what would be different about this project? How could we distinguish it from Dr Morwe's study? I enthusiastically replied, "Wellbeing," and that is how this project emerged. Given that I was a postdoc at the HSRC at the time, I was added to the project in this capacity. To strengthen the study further and link it with some of the work Prof. Luescher was already involved in through the Mellon Project, we decided that the Photovoice methodology should be used. This was an innovative technique to enable participants to discuss difficult issues. I also decided that, given the wellbeing focus, we needed a World Café workshop that would be totally focused on the way forward. So, there it was: the project was awarded the grant, and we now had the gigantic job of committing to all that was proposed in our application. Of course, a lot changed in the actual implementation, as is expected in any project, but we attempted to ensure that most of the aims of the study were fulfilled by the close of the project, and others were exceeded.

Initially, as I was the postdoctoral fellow and later the project manager, the project was basically "my baby". I did not carry the baby alone, because I had capable support from the principal investigator and co-principal investigator, but a lot depended on me. To mention a few of my duties in the project, I had to initiate the ethics application, institutional permissions and recruitment, organise data collection and be part of the data gathering itself. Data gathering involved travelling to three institutions outside of the Western Cape, where I lived, and conducting the research at UWC itself. For most of these trips, I had to leave behind my little girl, who had been born in November 2018, just about when we received the acceptance email from the NRF. This meant

that right after my maternity leave, I was on the road! And when I wasn't on the road, I was in the office of our administrator, Ms Fraser, or the principal investigator, Prof. Luescher, talking and planning the project. Remember, it was my baby! My reaction was one of joy because I acquired a grant, but when I saw how much I needed to be away from home, I thought to myself, "What was I thinking!" But every trip was worth it. The research experience, the data gathered, the challenges, the interactions, are a compelling story we hope to tell you through this coffee table book!

It was also a big learning curve. Let me list all the things I learned. I got to visit parts of South Africa that I had never been to. I had the opportunity really to get a feel for the South African university landscape and understand student experiences in a way that was different for me compared with when I was a PhD student at SU. Needless to say, I got to learn to do Photovoice research, attempt to execute World Café workshops, and now write this book with my colleagues. I must say, it did push me out of my comfort zone, because working with Thierry requires one to think outside the box and be innovative. I really enjoyed our debriefing sessions, where we would come together to reflect on individual experiences of each research site.

As for an assessment of the project: it is my baby! I am not sure I can give an objective assessment. Did we fail at times? Yes! Did we have some wins? Definitely! For instance, UWC was a near debacle. It almost did not work out. But, hey, we learned from it and lowered our expectations. We figured out better recruitment strategies and how to encourage participants to stay for the duration of the project. Organisation was difficult sometimes, as we had to liaise with people via email and phone and patiently wait for feedback, but did we achieve our aims? It is a definite yes! What did I enjoy most? The hotels and the food! No, just kidding, I enjoyed talking to students. I learned so much from them, because they gave me a lot to think about. What could we have done better? Planning! You can never plan enough. And perhaps figure out how to execute a World Café in a better way!

Hopes for the project: I am a researcher, and so my first desire is to get this information out there. Make it accessible! Students, professionals, academics, government, university management – they need to read this book! It is also good archival data that others can look back on in telling the story of the student movement in South Africa. Of course, more publications! And, lastly, to build on this work through intervention research.

MS TANIA FRASER, HSRC, CAPE TOWN

I was fortunate enough to be part of this project from its conception, and working with a motley crew of researchers from the get-go only contributed to the richness of the experience. I remember reading the research proposal and being struck how different this was to other projects

I had administered – not only because of the Photovoice methodology, but rather the subject matter, which transported me to my youth. I grew up on the Cape Flats, and my contribution to the "struggle" was throwing a single stone at a Casspir parked outside my school. I missed.

A state of emergency was declared, and school closed for the remainder of the year. Suppressing traumatic events as a coping measure was par for the course, yet I remember the tension, the uncertainty, the talks of civil war, the Trojan Horse incident that happened not too far from my home, and Ashley Kriel's death. But we weren't allowed to talk politics at home.

Things came to a head, though, when I received the Sacrament of Holy Confirmation. I was so excited, as I was now deemed to be an adult in the church. That meant church attendance would be voluntary and sleeping in on Sunday mornings was now possible. I remember walking out of church, smiling, happy, and looking forward to a special lunch. And there it was. A hippo parked on the church grounds with soldiers in full combat gear, rifles slung across their chests. This is an illegal gathering, they told us. How dare they? This is sacred ground, and you're desecrating it with your ugly brutality, I thought. I was angry.

So, when the research group gathered in November 2020 and we pored over photos taken by students, I recognised the frustration, anger, and betrayal. What I didn't understand was the destruction that accompanied protests. I still don't. Perhaps this project will provide insight into this peculiarity, which is not confined only to student movements in South Africa; in that way, institutions worldwide could learn how to respond without compounding an already traumatic experience.

MS THALENTE HADEBE,
DUT, GREYVILLE

I am Thalente Hadebe, and I was born in Charles Johnson Memorial Hospital in Nquthu (KwaZulu-Natal). I was raised in the Madadeni township in Newcastle. I am the last born in my home; I have only an older sister (Nolwazi). We are just a small family. I finished my matric in 2015 at Amadada High School.

In 2016, I had to search for a university, since my applications were all late. I was a walk-in at DUT. Comrade Sphesihle Khumalo helped me to search for spaces in different departments at DUT. Fortunately enough, I was accepted to do a National Diploma in Sport Management, even though I did not have a sponsor or bursary. My mother, Nompumelelo G. Hadebe, was the only one who was responsible for my fees after I lost my father in 2009. I could not register for residence, since my mother could not afford it. I had to stay in the Umlazi township (Z section) in my church mates' place for the first semester. In the second semester, I looked for another place to stay around Umlazi. I moved to D section and rented there. I was using the train (Mnyandu station to Berea station) to travel to school, because it was cheaper. I had to wake up at 4:30 in the morning and leave the house at 5:30. It was a hard experience because sometimes I missed my lectures due to a train delay. During the second semester, I was financially excluded for two modules.

The SRC helped me to register for those two modules. Then the #FeesMustFall protest began. Activists from different political affiliations came into our classroom and asked us to join the #FeesMustFall protest, and I joined the movement. I joined the movement because I was also affected by the fee increment and financially excluded. I remember on the third day of #FeesMustFall, I became an activist, and I was elected onto the ANCYL Branch Executive Committee, Duma Nokwe Branch at DUT. It was quite a good experience; bear in mind, I was still a first-year. Then I was elected onto the SRC sub-committee for 2016/17. In 2017, I got an NSFAS grant, but I did not get residence due to the shortage of residences at our institution. As a result, NSFAS covered only my tuition fees. Then, I had to go back and stay in Umlazi again in my second year. Even though the situation was not easy for me, I made sure that I excelled in my schoolwork. As much as I was striking and joining the movement, I was still excelling in my schoolwork. In the second semester, I was assisted by the SRC president, Miss Zama Mncube, who arranged a place to stay in town.

Things became easier for me. I had a lot of time to focus on my schoolwork, attend all my lectures and participate in political programmes, such as the "Back to School Campaign". Then, in 2018, I was fully funded by NSFAS; they covered me for fees and accommodation. Then, in 2019, I graduated, but unfortunately I did not get my certificate because I had outstanding fees. I started my B. Tech in Business Administration and became a DUT SRC member for 2019/20 as Sport and Recreation Officer. In 2020, I finished my second qualification without getting any certificates, because I still owed fees. Unfortunately, on 7 January 2021, I lost my mother – my everything, my rock, my best friend, my support structure, the woman who had supported me throughout – whenever I had any problem, I always went home to her shoulder. She was a support system.

MR SPHELELE KHUMALO, CPUT, CAPE TOWN, CURRENTLY UNISA

I'm Sphelele Khumalo, from the rural areas of Mtubatuba, KwaMpukunyoni, in the province of KwaZulu-Natal. I joined the student movement about six years ago. To be honest, I joined the movement even before I actually signed my name on any membership forms; this was as a result of the task that our collective suffering has placed upon us – the task of freeing ourselves from all the shackles of suffering and terror placed upon us. Our collective suffering as young black people in such an inherently anti-black country makes us part of the gigantic movement with one great raison d'être: doing away with colonialism, i.e., decolonisation. It is Andile Mngxitama of the Black Consciousness Movement, BLF, who reminds us, "All black people are members of BLF." (For the interests of this short reflection, BLF extends to any movement or organisation that speaks to the interests of black people, the damned of the earth, so to speak.)

He constantly uttered this very important phrase as a reminder that as black people (young, old, educated, less educated, rich, poor), we collectively suffer from the same dagger of anti-blackness, and our liberation will come from the actions of our collectiveness in the struggle for justice and freedom. Heeding the call for freedom and justice through the decolonial cause, higher education students have identified their generational mission and placed their bodies on the line so as to fulfil it. I joined the student movement to be part of this history-changing cause. If we may recall, it is the late black theologian and father of Black Liberation Theology, Prof. Rev. James H. Cone, who pours wisdom upon us, the oppressed: that if we are to be free as black people, we will have to fight and get that freedom ourselves.

My dear sister, comrade and friend, Zaza, had been invited to be a participant in the project, and through her we learned that more participants were needed; that's how my friends and I got in. Although I was a bit sceptical at first, given the history of how student struggles are used by the so-called academics to seek promotion and write about them from a position of privilege, after the introductory session I knew for sure that this was a project where we as students would be active participants, which is very rare in our commodified academic spaces.

The project was a great success for two important reasons: (1) we learned about Photovoice, and (2) as students, we were given a chance to reflect on our experiences during and post the student movement protests. This allowed us to iron out some thoughts and feelings that had stayed inside us, unmoved, untouched but piling up like volcanoes waiting to explode just at the right time. Throughout the project, I had the feeling that even though things seemed normal in the long academic halls, normalcy was really a farce that spat on our heads as students, mostly black, whose bodies invited violence. The reason behind this feeling was an understanding that came to me from experience and observation, that violence against the students was not meted out just by the police force, running in the spirit of "law and order", but by an anti-black state that was willing to send young black students to early graves so as to keep the status quo intact.

My most enjoyable moment was the lunch! Hahaha! To be honest, it was nice. Sitting down with my dear brothers and sisters to speak about our traumas and suffering meant everything to me. It defined a moment that cannot be told of in any words. I saw faces of young black students who had gone out from home to universities for degrees, but had seen (and personally experienced) suffering, pain, and exclusion, and could not stand it. They organised themselves and set themselves against the reign of terror and evil. The project successfully gave us a platform to realise and share these moments of love – these precious moments, if I may.

I pray and hope that the book makes its way to the desks of policymakers in this country. They must know that until what they valorise as education in this anti-black country speaks to the interest of the majority population, it is not education, but rather "miseducation". Universities need to understand that they are not factories for producing corporate zombies, but a space for knowledge production. To those who put their bodies on the line, we say that one day, soon, the cycle of the South African education system is to be broken.

research team members, Dr Angelina Wilson Fadiji, as a candidate for occupying the position of a research intern on the project, as they were looking for an intern. Her recommendation was mainly informed by the fact that my research also focuses on the wellbeing of students, albeit on African international students and how the relationships they develop in their time in South Africa influence their wellbeing amid all the challenges they encounter.

When I was presented with the offer, I was very happy and agreed to be a part of the project without hesitation. My acceptance required little thought, given my general interest and previous involvement in research involving students (youth) and wellbeing. Furthermore, I saw it as a fantastic opportunity to gain new research skills and improve on my current research skills as a future research psychologist. Thus, I joined the violence and wellbeing project in mid-2020.

My overall experience in the project has been bittersweet. It has been an incredible opportunity working alongside my colleagues and learning, growing, and being challenged along the way, as I have put my theoretical knowledge into practice. However, as I was not actively involved in the 2015/16 #FeesMustFall movement, I did not understand the experience of the students closest to the movement. Although one could see through media the violence that was being inflicted upon students and the potential consequences, it does not compare with hearing about the aftermath of the #FeesMustFall protests from the students themselves. It was heartbreaking to hear students (even those not involved in the movement but nonetheless

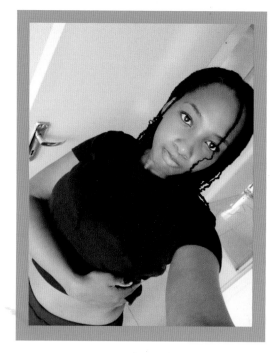

MS TSHIRELETSO S. LETSOALO, UP, PRETORIA

I am currently completing my final year for an MA in Research Psychology at UP. My supervisor, Dr Shingairai Chigeza, recommended me to one of the violence and wellbeing

affected) speak about the traumas they experienced that persist to this day – dreams shattered and lives lost – much of which, one realises, could have been avoided if university management had not waited for matters to escalate to violence before they granted students an audience or truly made an effort to listen to and address their issues.

My favourite moment in being part of the Violence and Wellbeing team was when we conducted the virtual Photovoice sessions, wherein students submitted pictures of their violence and wellbeing experiences and provided narratives to support the images. It was the only opportunity I had to engage with and hear the students directly, as I had joined the project in its late stages. It was not only enlightening, but it took place just after I had joined the project, and hearing about the students' experiences gave me the vigour necessary to participate in the project meaningfully. I hope that from this book, people might empathise more with student experiences and student activists, seeing them less as violent hooligans and more as young individuals fighting for a noble cause that can lead to necessary and positive changes in South African higher education institutions.

PROF. THIERRY M. LUESCHER, HSRC, CAPE TOWN

I arrived in Alice on the hot summer Sunday evening of 23 February 2020, just a month before the country went into its first and hardest COVID lockdown. After I had checked into the homely Sangweni bed and breakfast, we all met up in Dr Angelina Wilson Fadiji's rondavel to discuss our programme for the next five days. Antonio Erasmus, who always led the training workshops in photography and photographic ethics with the students, had come up from Cape Town with me. Dr Keamo Morwe had just travelled almost 1 500 km from Univen in Thohoyandou to the Eastern Cape. Angelina had set up to brief us, but we already knew from our WhatsApp group with the student leaders of UFH that doing the Photovoice workshops that week was going to be difficult.

Campus was under siege. All the gates were manned by armed security guards in riot gear, while inside the campus, students had gathered for a funeral service, and there was chatter of a shutdown for the week. On Monday, as we climbed the heavy stone stairs to the Centre for Leadership Ethics in Africa in the Stewart Building, we could see and hear through the windows distant protestors and security guards giving each other their best.

The Violence and Wellbeing project sprang from the confluence of several opportunities. One was Dr Angelina Wilson Fadiji joining the HSRC in July 2017 with her specialist training in Positive Psychology and Wellbeing Studies. Another was my work with Dr Keamogetse Morwe, whose original training was as a social worker and who did her PhD under my co-supervision on violence in the student movement. And then there was my own interest in student politics and the #FeesMustFall movement in particular, as well as a worry I was carrying around with me.

For the larger research project, which collected the reflections of former student activists on their participation in #RhodesMustFall, #FeesMustFall, and related campus movements and campaigns, I had conducted over 50 interviews, mostly one on one, face to face, with student activists across the country. In too many sittings, I was confronted with psychological and emotional scars lingering in the aftermath of their exposure to violence. One of the former student leaders I had gotten to know a few years earlier while working at UFS was the former chairperson of Tswelopele residence, Tshepang Mahlatsi. Unlike most others, who rather internalised their trauma

from police brutality, he had confronted his demons and, after a year of battling depression, had started the student-run psychological support group, Next Chapter, at UFS. The NRF Human and Social Dynamics call for proposals of 2018 provided me with the opportunity to work with former student activists and my expert colleagues and, with reference to the students' and our own experiences, address questions of violence and post-violence wellbeing, create awareness and new knowledge, and hopefully effect some change for the better.

I had been a student leader at UCT 20 years earlier and participated in many protest marches – mostly to demonstrate against the academic and financial exclusion of students. As vice-president of the Students' Representative Council in 1999/2000, I had also had students confide in me their experiences of racism and sexism. It was part of my role to confront the perpetrators and report the incidents to the relevant university offices and in meetings with the management. University management may have been unhelpful at times, but never condescending, unresponsive or, even worse, absent. And I never had to confront police officers or security guards who were out to cause pain rather than prevent it. In my day, their role was to protect us, the protestors, to allow us to exercise that newly won democratic right. Over the years, my role naturally morphed from being a political activist in higher education to becoming a researcher on such. Those experiences I had in the UCT SRC stayed with me, and now, working with an entirely new generation of student leaders, I could see myself in them and empathise, and I was able to understand why they acted as they did when so much more still needed to change.

Perhaps it helped that I did not grow up in an apartheid society and had not experienced the extreme privileges a white boy born in the 1970s would have had in South Africa. I grew up a working-class kid in rural Switzerland. In a mono-racial community, one's skin colour is pretty inconsequential; my "misfortune", rather, was to have hair bright as a fox's tail, and that was enough to put me on any bully's hit list. Once puberty began, my luck doubled with an attraction to the wrong gender. In retrospect, working through internalised homophobia was considerably harder than dealing with the odd bigot. Part of my process here was to politicise this part of my identity early on in my adult life – and so I found the emancipatory identity politics which I encountered in South Africa, and the material and psychological struggle dimensions thereof, normal, necessary, and part of my own.

Ever since I was in the SRC, I have had a soft spot for the students of Univen. The first time I visited Univen, I was the guest speaker at their Student Assembly opening in August 2000. The Univen SRC treasurer, Prince Mashele, had invited me for this honour, and the campus and its students reminded me of my days at the University of Ghana years earlier. When we did the Photovoice workshops with the students at Univen in 2019, I often couldn't figure out whether I was amazed or extremely angry. Nineteen years after my first visit to Univen, the campus looked only marginally better, with a couple new buildings. But its political climate had deteriorated in its

disunity with party politics: the ANCYL, YCL, and SASCO in their uneasy alliance opposing the red berets of the EFF and Democratic Alliance Student Organisation students in blue T-shirts. But worse than the partisan antagonism was the students' glorification of violence on the campus.

Univen is placed in an idyllic, seemingly peaceful, subtropical setting. The master's student intern on the project from Univen, Kulani Mlambo, had to spend much time explicating for us what the heck was going on here. The pictures that students excavated from their online archives and took on their campus rounds were staggering. As much as they joked and laughed in the Photovoice workshops when talking about their photos and recounting their experiences, in effect they described a student body that was para-militarised – even if this was still rudimentary. There was the "supplies department", the male "frontline" soldiers and the female "backliners"; there were the cooks and the nurses, who ensured that the activists were in good health and motivated for battle, and even a "stone department" that ensured that protestors had adequate provision of bricks as ammunition. Though rife at any other moment, in the heat of protest, party affiliation moved to the background, and the activists stood together to defend their campus on the bridge at Golgotha against police incursion.

In 2020, Tshireletso Letsoalo joined the core research team as a master's student from UP's Psychology Department. She was key in helping us move our project online, so that our efforts would not be defeated by the COVID-19 lockdown. We had started reflecting on our

Rapid Photovoice research method, but taking it to Zoom presented a new challenge and experience. Eventually, in July 2020, we met for three days online with student leaders and activists from DUT, working with them through their lived experiences of violence and struggles to restore wellbeing in the aftermath of the #FeesMustFall protests.

Then, with the help of renowned journalist and photographer Carl Collison, the photo exhibitions that the students from the five universities had created in the course of 2019/20 were curated into a single online exhibition. Omar Badsha, who had been an enthusiastic supporter of the student movement project from its inception, made sure that SAHO came to host the online exhibition in December 2020.

In this project, we aim to recount the message of the students, to labour for their cries to be heard and to offer platforms to let them tell their stories. But, despite so many photo exhibitions, talks, articles and seminars, it still is difficult to convey their experiences. We hold workshops with university leaders, present at the national higher education leadership conferences, and hold seminars with Student Affairs managers and counselling staff, with student participants of our project present in most cases. We have not only taken the exhibition online, but criss-crossed the country with it and even heeded the invitation to host it at the University of Botswana in Gaborone. Yet there remains the nagging uncertainty of whether we will positively contribute to changing the trajectory of a seemingly deteriorating university-student relationship. I hope, with my colleagues and many of the former student leaders and activists who participated in this project, that

there will come a time when the political structures will be transformed to a point where an ordinary student, as much as a student representative, will be heard and responded to without delay; a time when this country will have made its long-awaited great leap forward to true democracy and allowed a share in its prosperity for all; and thus a time when the stakes will have become so low that student politics will be boring.

DR KEAMOGETSE G. MORWE, UNIVEN, THOHOYANDOU

I am Keamogetse G. Morwe. I was born and raised in Mabopane, a township outside Pretoria, and I am the only daughter in a family of three. I matriculated in 1991 at Ngaka Maseko High School, and, knowing that I did not have a bursary, I decided in 1992 to fundraise for university. In 1993,

I was accepted at the former University of Bophuthatswana (Unibo), currently the North-West University (NWU), to study social work. I chose Unibo out of national pride: the Batswana contributed to its construction, and since my father was born in Mahikeng, it was home. Of course, fees were another consideration, because the Batswana paid registration fees. However, I received a Kagiso Trust bursary, 40 percent of which was a loan. I remember how my friend Kagiso Kaise and I sat on the pavement and became proxy parents (I was her mother, and she mine), because we knew there was no other viable option.

Three months into my being a university student, Mr. Chris Hani was assassinated. The fear that gripped the community was immeasurable. There was so much uncertainty and confusion. One moment, we'd learn that lectures were cancelled, and a few minutes later there was a radio announcement that they had resumed. One fateful day, Ivy and I decided to go into town at Mahikeng; on our return, while in the taxi, we heard a report that lectures had resumed. When we alighted, we ran our lungs out because we had a test to write that day. Luckily, there were no lectures. Despite the tensions in the country, the situation calmed down and life returned to normal.

That same year, the ANC was on a campaign trail, and both former president Mandela and Mrs Winnie Mandela came to Mmabatho, the former to the stadium and the latter to the university's great hall. That year, it was apparent that there would be a political transition, especially since Mr Mangope refused to be part of the transitional talks. By 1994, the situation was untenable, and there were student-led protests. In all of these protests, we would gather at the main gate and sing struggle songs, with an occasional blocking of the road. Whatever happened then, we never damaged our university. Perhaps apart from identifying with the university, we knew what would befall us should we be caught. One day, while we were protesting, a hippo chased Ivy, Kealebetswe, and me. We ran non-stop to someone's home (Mr Thapelo Thipe's, I think), closed ourselves in the main bedroom (farthest room) and lay still on the floor. Despite the commotion we caused, we were welcome to stay as long as we were comfortable, before returning to the residences. The events of the weeks that followed are fuzzy because I never revisited them.

In March, Mr Mangope was deposed. Fear gripped us. I remember resident students having meetings with the SRC leaders, who warned us not to drink the water as it might be poisoned. Police and soldiers were everywhere. It became apparent that Mr Mangope had lost power, and looting began. Mangope was gone. In 1996, I completed my studies, but on my graduation in 1997, I received a statement of account instead of a certificate, putting a damper on my achievement. Ironically, I received the Merit Award certificate.

I started working in 1997 and joined the academy in 2003 at Technikon South Africa, Florida campus, now the University of South Africa. A year later, I joined the Institute for Youth Studies at Univen, where I am currently based. Over the years, I observed that our students destroyed university property each time they protested. When I asked why they did this, the response was that our government reacts to violence. This observation sparked my research interest.

My proposed PhD research question became why South African university students resort to violence when they have problems with authority. With such a controversial research question, I struggled to get a supervisor. My resolve not to get a terminal degree from another historically black university fuelled the challenge. In 2014, I received an Erasmus Mundus scholarship through Univen to study at the University of Málaga, Spain. In 2016, my supervisor, Prof. Elisa Garcia-España, shared that I needed to have a South African supervisor. That is how I met Prof. Thierry Luescher, who was then at UFS.

I got involved with the project in 2018 after discussions with Professor Thierry Luescher and Dr Angelina Fadiji, the project manager. I was a bit apprehensive about being part of a project that researched violence, because my data collection process had been traumatic, and I had not dealt with this. I found comfort in that our project would infuse healing elements because it took a wellbeing approach. Most attractive about the project was its innovative data methods: Photovoice and World Café. Therefore, I was not going to pass on an opportunity to learn. Although I had doubts, when I realised that the proposal for funding had an excerpt of what I had written, I became confident that whatever challenges I encountered, I would be well.

The success of the project depended on three individuals, two with a dreamy disposition and another who is strict – however, all passionate about their craft. Therefore, it was crucial that we were adequately prepared, from getting interns to attending training sessions about the research methods and requesting permission from proposed sites. The actual implementation of the project had its challenges, despite all our efforts to ensure that loopholes were dealt with. Despite the lack of support from some quarters, it was always wonderful to see the student activists warming up to us and trusting us with their stories. While the content that we discussed was heavy, the use of pictures, which depicted both violence and resources for coping, helped me to realise that despite the challenges encountered, student activists provided one another with the necessary support. Further, the project provided the activists with an opportunity to ventilate their pent-up emotions, which they acknowledged had never been expressed. Hearing the activists appreciating the opportunity to express and reflect on their feelings, thoughts, and actions in a non-judgmental space was remarkable. The World Café sessions were also crucial, because they were a platform for student activists and university staff (Student Affairs practitionaers, academics, and administrators) to engage one another and chart strategies for less confrontational engagement.

Our book aims to present an untold story to the university stakeholders and the public at large. Therefore, I hope that those who come across it see the brutality of violence toward the student protestors as meted out by the authorities and other students – but also realise that there are non-brutalising ways to engage, as violence harms all the parties concerned.

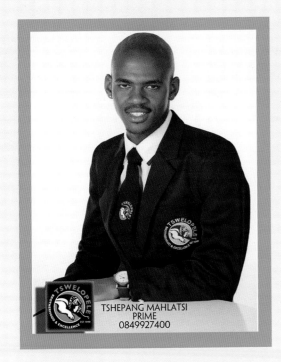

TSHEPANG MAHLATSI
PRIME
0849927400

MR TSHEPANG MAHLATSI, UFS, BLOEMFONTEIN

My name is Tshepang Mahlatsi, and I was raised in Tumahole Parys in the Free State, where I started school and matriculated in 2013. In 2014, I enrolled for a Bachelor of Laws degree (LLB), conferred in 2021. Currently, I am pursuing a Master of Laws degree specialising in Mercantile Law at UFS.

Tumahole is a township rich in history with many struggle heroes who played a critical role in the fight against apartheid in South Africa. Some of our heroes documented in mainstream history include Ace Magashule, secretary-general of the African National Congress. Fezile Dabi was instrumental in the formation of some progressive organisations which challenged the apartheid government in South Africa. Stompie Seipei was a 14- or 15-year-old comrade whose story was crucial in the TRC, where Winnie Mandela was at the centre of the allegations of his murder.

I attended three schools in Tumahole Parys: AM Lembede Primary School, Aha Sechaba Primary (to complete my grade seven), and Barnard Molokoane Comprehensive School. Two of these schools, AM Lembede and Barnard Molokoane, are named after instrumental figures who contributed immensely to the fight against apartheid in South Africa. AM Lembede, founding president of the African National Congress Youth League, and Barnard Molokoane, an MK operative, were assassinated during the struggle.

In my secondary school years and even my university years, I have always identified as an apolitical individual. I have never wanted to be affiliated with any political organisation. I have always wanted to maintain my independent views on politics and agree with what makes sense, using my judgment more than organisational patriotism and loyalty. In most cases, this view has constantly been challenged and I have been misunderstood for never taking on the constitutional duty of participating in elections or political discourse; however, these views are not accurate.

Interestingly, I have always found myself in leadership positions; at Barnard Molokoane, I was elected president of the Representative Council of Learners (RCL) in 2012 and secretary of the RCL in 2013. In both years, by virtue of my office, I served on the School Governing Body (SGB).

At UFS, I served on various student bodies, from residence to campus-based organisations. I served as the chairperson and research education facilitator for Students for Law and Social Justice (SLSJ) on campus. SLSJ is a South African student organisation dedicated to protecting human rights, preventing discrimination, and promoting social justice and the rule of law. It is a society formed in partnership between students of various universities in South Africa, and it is within the SLSJ that we aim to transform legal education and access to justice.

In residence, I served as the "Prime" (or head student) of House Tswelopele, a predominantly black male student residence on the UFS campus. In 2016, during the #FeesMustFall and #OutsourcingMustFall campaigns, and particularly in the week following the #ShimlaPark attack of racist violence exerted by white rugby spectators on black protestors, the Tswelopele residence was one of the "crime scenes". Members of the SAPS and private security were instructed to raid the residence so as to arrest student leaders. During the arrests, the residence was vandalised, teargas was thrown around, and students were manhandled and beaten by the police.

During all these movements, as a student leader, one had no choice but to provide leadership. The national momentum of the #FeesMustFall movement called for unity and mobilisation from anyone with influence or a position of leadership in the student communities, because the system was not so kind to students. To this day, some of us are still battling with permanent scars resulting from our involvement. University managements expelled some students, some expelled students lost their lives, and some suffered psychological damage like depression and post-traumatic stress disorder, as I did.

In 2019, after a series of engagements with my comrade and mentor, Prof. Luescher, I expressed my interest in narrating my involvement in the movement, the series of events, and the impact of the aftermath of violent protests on my psychological wellbeing and resultantly on my academics. In October 2019, the research team working with Prof. Luescher invited me to be a participant in the study, "Exploring the experience of violence and aggression in the wake of the 2015/16 student movement using a psychological wellbeing perspective."

I must say, I had mixed feelings about participating in the study. The initial feelings were a trauma response: that I would be opening myself up to be victimised by the university again, since it would be like I was exposing them. Secondly, I feared incriminating myself and putting myself at risk of universities instituting claims or litigations against me or other students based on what I shared. On the other hand, I was excited to be part of the study, because this study would form part of the future guideline for universities to consider when dealing with campus protests. I wanted to share my story as a case study of the failure of both students and university management to find common ground in situations that require engagement. Violence does permanent damage to what they are trying to protect: students and property.

To me, this whole project was "the meeting of the triggers". But I also realised that I was not the only one who had not come to terms with how the violent protests on campus had affected me. There is so much healing needed. There is a lack of accountability, and there are lives that are still to be accounted for. Some hopes are to be buried because the damage is far more significant. There is so much to mourn, and still there is so much to unearth. The violence and trauma still linger. During this process, I realised that in the eyes of participants, "the post-mortem was rushed, and that's why students have not healed". We speak and participate in such projects because we hope that the more we talk and engage, the more we will find the only form of inquest we have, to make peace with the question: "Was there a need for such violence?"

Had I not participated in this project, I would not have known how much I needed to confront myself and the violent spaces like our university. Inasmuch as it was re-traumatising, I enjoy the fact that I somewhat had an opportunity to look at everything from the point of: "Now that we are here, what could have been done differently?" I got to realise that I had issues with specific spaces, objects, languages, names, and signs around campus. I enjoyed telling the stories with people who had the same feelings. This project taught me the importance of the "single story – different trauma" notion. We are healing and doing so in different ways.

I hope that all student leaders will read these stories and think that the cause is worth taking. Where there is a need to provide leadership, they must. However, they always need to remember and invest in the art of engagement. Violence should never be the first move on the table. They must remember that students will become the victims of the system that always wins.

MS KULANI BONGIWE MLAMBO, UNIVEN, THOHOYANDOU

My name is Kulani Bongiwe Mlambo, and I am a former student of Univen. At the time of the project, I was still a master's student studying in the field of youth and development. I developed an interest in the project because it was youth-based, and at the time I was also politically active. I knew I had a lot to learn from this, which I would get from all the different parties involved. It was an exciting opportunity. The project came through my lecturer, Dr Morwe, who happened to be my supervisor, in the form of a scholarship. This was excellent news to me. It was my first time being given a scholarship, and to top it all, it was a scholarship project that was in my field of interest. It was a very proud moment for me, and it's rare to be given such chances in life.

The project was very educational. I learnt a lot from the team and all the parties involved. It was a straightforward project with no complications. It was easier when I had to listen to other people's experiences, but sharing mine was a bit uncomfortable – having to remember the experiences I went through during my time as an activist, having to take my mind back to the violence students suffered at the hands of the law, and the consequences that we had after the protests – it was excruciating. But the strength in it was that I was not alone. Many of us student activists had gone through the same ordeal. It gave me the conviction that we did the right things, and we should be proud of ourselves.

I enjoyed Photovoice. It was very interesting taking pictures and sharing our moments, when we would give meaning to the pictures, reflecting on those days and relating those memories to one another. In my understanding, we were creating memories that would not die with us, memories that generations will learn about even when we are gone.

For me, the uncomfortable part was when we had to take turns and talk. I believe that some things are better left unsaid, because psychologically I was fragile.

My expectations were exceedingly met. I am proud knowing I have been part of a very well-established project, and I have gained a lot of knowledge.

My hope for the project is that it grows beyond expectations and becomes accessible to all. The project will educate many people, including student activists, on how to deal with situations like these, if the need arises. It will give them strength to carry on even after violence. People will be able to get strategies on how to deal with aggression. The project is not giving them a manual, but hopefully they can always refer to it when there is a need.

MS SEIPATI MOKHEMA, HSRC CAPE TOWN, CURRENTLY WITS

My name is Seipati Mokhema. I am a student from NWU and until December 2021, I worked as a junior researcher at the HSRC. I witnessed the unrests that happened at my university's Mahikeng campus from October 2015 well into 2016 as students had been experiencing a range of problems like academic and financial exclusion, maladministration, and lack of adequate campus resources. The problems we had on our campus were greater in comparison to our sister campus in Potchefstroom.

I came to be a part of the violence and wellbeing project through an internship program at the HSRC. Initially, research work behind the project was a part of my job description but as soon as I got involved, I started to relate to all the students' stories as I too witnessed the protests at my former university and was also a victim of the violence that ensued on campus. I initially felt overwhelmed by the project because it brought up memories I chose to forget, but being involved proved to be more therapeutic as I learnt I was not alone in my trauma.

Being a part of the project afforded me the opportunity to reflect on my experience of violence and being violated and I now understand how those experiences have shaped how I respond to violence. I have learnt that I am a product of a system that is beyond my comprehension and, to a large extent, I was a helpless victim to violence. My reaction to the violence was thus a part of dissatisfaction of the current state of affairs along with millions of other South African students. I enjoyed being a part of the research background team as it exposed a lot more than I had seen and understood during my days as a student protestor. My least favourite part was listening to other students recount their memories of violence in the wake of the

#FeesMustFall movement, #RUReferenceList, and NSFAS related protests. These forced me to relive my own past traumatic experience related to violence at my university's campus. I am however looking forward to the long-term ripple effects the project will make.

I simply hope this book will tell stories that people chose to forget and unsee and it serves as a reminder that we will keep going in violent circles until we address the root cause of our problems as a people.

MS DIMAKATSO PATRICIA NGOBENI, UNIVEN, THOHOYANDOU

I am Dimakatso Patricia Ngobeni, also known as Dim-Dim. The name became familiar at Univen during the time I was a student. I was given the name by members of my organisation, which was ANCYL before they fell under the Progressive Youth Alliance. I was born and raised in Hlaneki village on the outskirts of Giyani, under the greater Giyani municipality in the Mopani district. I matriculated in 2001 and was unable to further my studies, because my parents were unable to afford my fees to study at any varsity of my choice, until one of the girls from my village shared some information about bursaries with us. I went to varsity after a full ten years after school. I decided to go to university to further my studies and to focus only on my academic studies, but unfortunately life at university was not all about academics. We had a lot of leisure time to refresh our minds, and one of the activities was politics. Singing those mzabalazo [protest] songs was very much unique and made one aspire to join politics full-time. I applied at Univen in 2011, and was admitted in 2012 on 11 February. I wanted to study a Bachelor of Social Work, and my second choice was psychology. Due to my low marks from matric, I did not reach the requirements and I had to start a BCom Accounting degree. In 2013, I had to change my degree to social work. Unfortunately, Univen was not admitting students to social work degrees that year, due to some accreditation issue with the South African Qualifications Authority. Then I opted for a Bachelor of Arts (Youth in Development), and hoped to change in 2014 when the Social Work department would admit students. But, because I fell in love with the modules that were taught in the BA degree, I continued with it until December 2016.

In March 2012, one of the senior students invited us to attend the Branch General Meeting of the ANCYL, where he was contesting for secretary. He was looking for support from us, and the guy came to us because he heard us speaking Xitsonga, and he was also a Tsonga. We went there to support him, and from that day my heart fell in love with the atmosphere and the songs that the comrades were singing. Now, I had left home not being a fan of any political party. Univen is a rural university, where the majority of students are using NSFAS and bursaries, so it was difficult when students had to strike, because the majority would be on the street while the minority who were using cash would be chanting that they wanted to go back to classes. I still remember very well, in 2012, the first strike was about students not receiving their food and book allowances in time, while in other universities students received everything immediately after registration. The strike was organised by a group of Azanian People's Organisation comrades, who later burned the university tuck shop, and seven students were arrested. Immediately after the arrests, students were afraid to continue with their strikes, and this made the university run their business as usual.

I was invited by my former lecturer, Dr Morwe, to be one of the participants of this project, since she knows me very well and knows that I was very active in politics, and that I love to share ideas with people, and she knew that I am good at communication and interacting with anyone. I was very excited to be part of this project, because I love student politics with all my heart. The fact that all my political organisations would be there and be exchanging views made me excited, and I did not want to miss this opportunity. I also found the topic "Violence and well-being" very interesting, as they were talking about the strikes that university students were conducting, whether illegal or legal, and in all the strikes during my time as a student, I had been at the forefront. The student protests are a major manifestation of the shortcomings and failures of the transformation of South Africa's higher education. They have also emerged as an illustration of expanding frustration with the state of South Africa, its extreme inequalities, its widespread poverty, and its huge youth unemployment. Social protests and community action have been a feature of South African politics for many years, but the student protests were the first major national wave of protests.

For me, to be part of this project was just to reflect on memories from my days as a student, and I enjoyed reflecting on all the memories we had at Univen. Students at Univen suffered a lot, because the services that they got from financial offices were very bad compared with those at other universities. I still remember, we used to be given Intel Cards, with our meal and book allowance, in November when we were done writing our exams. A person would suffer the whole year and only get their allowance in December, when the money would no longer serve any purpose. Students used to sell their grocery tickets for cash to travel home with, as the cards only worked at Thohoyandou and not in other towns or cities. The system changed when students stood up to strike against financial officers and management, and everything was fixed because students exposed management in the media with the strike.

After completing my studies and reflecting, I found all the memories very emotional. Most of the things we used to do during strikes were not necessary. After all, they also sabotaged our services as students, such as by burning the laundry service, which assisted most of the people on campus, especially male students, because most of them can't wash for themselves, and ironically, in most cases, they lead the strike. I experienced that the strikes affected students with disabilities, as their lives were put in more danger than ours, since we could run away when the police were chasing us and also when the police were throwing teargas. Some of the students dropped out of school because of the charges that universities had against them. It is so painful, because when we are striking, we are united, but once others are arrested, all of us start to focus on our studies and leave those with whom we struggled together, to burn alone in the fire that we all started. In most cases, when students are striking, we use this motto: "An injury to one is an injury to all," but when the police come, we start distancing ourselves from such a slogan. As a South African, I think we can do better by engaging with relevant stakeholders than by acting like illiterate people who are unaware of the consequences of violent strikes. Being a student means you are an intellectual and you can think beyond the current situation. Students' voices must be heard in debates or dialogues, not through strikes.

Not knowing the true stories, one can easily misjudge the actions and frustrations.

MR ALDO BRINCAT, STELLENBOSCH UNIVERSITY, CAPE TOWN

To my knowledge, as I write this, I am the newest addition to the HSRC family and its "Violence and Wellbeing in the Context of the Student Movement" project.

I came to this project on the coat-tails of my husband, the curator of the "Aftermath" exhibition, Carl Collison. While he curated this exhibition in our tiny Cape Town apartment, a stone's throw away from UCT, I became increasingly informed of – and engrossed by – the events and nuances of the #FeesMustFall movement.

Then an opportunity presented itself for me to offer my services in the actual hardware and logistics of printing, mounting, chaperoning, and touring this exhibition.

I drew on my experience of having produced a similar body of work while living in Botswana, where I lived for 12 years and worked as a high school teacher. In my spare time – over a period of two years – I worked on a photobook (published by African Scripts) and a travelling exhibition. So, there were many similarities to this project when it came to logistics.

Living and working in Botswana was a powerful formative experience. Having South Africa as its wild cousin across the border is an intense experience. Botswana has a love-hate relationship with South Africa, with many people having intertwined families, histories, and business interests. South Africa's roller coaster of events (almost on a daily basis) provided us with moments of humour and horror.

The University of Botswana has its own history of student protest: while they have been mostly peaceful, there has been an increasing tendency for armed forces to find their way onto campus at various times – a trend that (to my knowledge) has been widely condemned by the citizens of Botswana.

I should cut across at this point and let you know that I myself was only recently a first-time South African university student, completing my postgraduate degree at UCT (2020). I am now a master's student at SU (2021).

I have noted with interest the service I receive as a mature white man, compared with black students. I have also found myself facing a fair amount of stonewalling from university administration, which I believe has nothing to do with my identity as a mature white man, but rather arise from the machinations of a university system that is founded on principles of financial profit, facilitated by the omniscient presence of technology.

My first-time South African university experience (2020) coincided with the "Aftermath" exhibition and with the shutting of university campuses due to the COVID-19 pandemic and its attendant lockdowns. The surge of online teaching at UCT, in my opinion, failed dismally to provide online content worthy of the university's world-class status. Despite this, the institution acted with impunity in maintaining their demands for full fees in a devastating economic climate.

The global move to digitising all forms of communications seems to lock out anyone who simply wants to "talk" about any dissatisfaction. We were subjected to all this "stonewalling" while simultaneously receiving a relentless stream of "upbeat" newsletters from UCT featuring a barrage of patronising instructions on how to deal with COVID.

That was last year.

I was delighted beyond words that the "Aftermath" exhibition's first proper engagement with a university was to be at the University of Botswana in October 2021. And I was curious as to how a not-so-foreign student body and faculty would react to seeing the "shenanigans" of their cousins across the border.

One cannot begin to imagine or explain what a mostly non-colonial and non-weaponised university experience can be until one sets foot into the University of Botswana.

Back in the day, under the inspired leadership of the second president, His Excellency Ketumile Quett Masire, the people decided to build a university for the people. For years, Sunday broadcasts on the radio would be devoted to reading a list of donations from the people, be it money, a load of bricks, a crate of tea, or even livestock for the nourishment of the builders. Every contribution was noted, celebrated, and read out with gratitude and pride. Indeed, to this day, there is a marvellous bronze sculpture at the entrance of the university library, of a humble farmer herding a cow to the university grounds.

It really seems that everyone is on the same page at the University of Botswana, from the cleaners and security guards to the lecturers and students. This is in sharp contrast to my experience at UCT. For me, the general feeling at UCT was that of mistrust, suspicion, greed, and an unspoken violence that seems to be on constant boil just under the surface.

I was educated by the response of University of Botswana students to the "Aftermath" exhibition. They were curious, informed, knowledgeable, and defiant. In many of the conversations, there was an underlying sentiment of either smugness or alarm at some of the images: a kind of "Thank God that's not us" or "They must not think they can bring 'that shit' here."

There are two images from the exhibition that the students from the University of Botswana really seemed to respond to during my few days there as a chaperone and observer. The first one is of a young male student who was shot with rubber bullets. His wounds were so extensive that he passed on a few days later – a stark reminder that when we say "rubber bullets", we are not talking about a gun shooting Hello Kitty pencil erasers. The horror that a robust young man might actually die from wounds sustained at your local suburban university at the hands of a police force, seemed incomprehensible and immensely tragic to them. And rightly so.

The second image is a snapshot of a transcript recording a student's annual study results. The early recordings indicate that the student in question is a model student, with a listing of distinction after distinction. As the year and #FeesMustFall gathers momentum, the grades dwindle down to a pass, and then on to an abyss of incomplete and, ultimately, fail. It is a haunting image. No face, no apparent violence. One can say, in this image, that the violence against black bodies becomes encrypted. The subliminal trauma is plain for all to see. The image is almost a piece of theatre.

My work as a master's art student at SU centres on notions of encryption, monumentalisation, commemoration, landscape, and language. I seek to understand past trauma and how to inhabit it today. One of my own pieces closest to my heart, titled "The Freedom Charter", calls us to remember the basics upon which our country is founded. In this piece, the entire Freedom Charter is encrypted, spelled out with

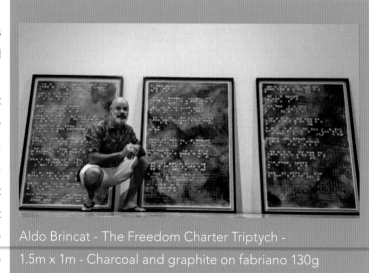

Aldo Brincat - The Freedom Charter Triptych - 1.5m x 1m - Charcoal and graphite on fabriano 130g

drawings of small stones and laid out in Braille formation. The piece is then framed behind glass. My intention is that seeing people cannot understand the text as it is laid out in Braille formation – and visually impaired people cannot read it with their fingertips either, as it is laid out behind a sheet of glass.

The Freedom Charter first came to my attention as a young layman, when I attended protests at the Durban Ecumenical Centre back in the mid-'80s. This important document was coupled with a religious text, The Beatitudes (commonly known as "Jesus' Sermon on the Mount"). As the Freedom Charter was the cornerstone of a new South African Constitution, so the Beatitudes were the cornerstone of anyone wanting to call themselves a follower of Christ. What I adored about these two documents was that, despite the one being secular and the other religious, both spoke to the same issues: welcoming all to a society free of discrimination and suffering, one of equality and equal access. They are both idealistic by today's standards, but

30 years ago they were the "power couple" of the freedom struggle. Hence my encrypting of the Freedom Charter: it has fallen on deaf ears.

I would encourage us all to take a moment and reread the Freedom Charter. And to do so out loud to each other. It's only a few sentences long. Let it sink in. Let the disparity between reality and ideal sink in. As you read, let the images of police weapons and bruised student bodies sink in.

When I stood in the vast foyer of the University of Botswana Library, the mid-spring sunlight pouring in through gigantic windows, the "Aftermath" exhibition filling a wall at my side, I was filled with a deep, melancholic pathos. Botswana has its problems, and the University of Botswana is not exempt from its own flavour of tertiary blues. But fundamentally, what is central in this matter is profound ownership – deep, intrinsic, and fundamental ownership by the people, for the people.

BOTSWANA EXHIBITION

PHOTO INDEX

pp. 46, 76: supplied by NRF project team, published with permission of Ashraf Hendricks.

pp. 165, 166: supplied by Keamogetse G. Morwe, published with permission of Keamogetse G. Morwe.

pp. 24: supplied by Sphelele Khumalo

pp. 10, 24, 45, 90, 103, 122, 126: supplied by NRF project team, Tshepang Mahlatsi, and Kamohelo Maphike and published with the permission of Lihlumelo Toyana.

pp. 58, 73: supplied by Siyasanga Ndwayi and published with the permission of Luxolo Mlunguza.

pp. xviii: supplied by NRF project team and published with the permission of Nicholas Rawhani.

pp. 20: supplied by NRF project team and published with the permission of UKZN Press.

pp. 8, 82, 106, 114, 150, 159: supplied by Thierry M. Luescher and published with the permission of Thierry M. Luescher.

Front cover and pp. ii, v, 42, 62, 108, 142, 160, 163: supplied by NRF project team, Siyasanga Ndwayi, Asandiswa Bomvana, Kamohelo Maphike, and Azania Simthandile Tyhali and published with the permission of Wandile Kasibe.

pp. 49: supplied by Abednego Sam Mandhlazi

pp. 22: supplied by Akhona Manyenyeza

pp. 188, 190: supplied by Aldo Brincat

pp. 168: supplied by Angelina Wilson Fadiji

pp. 28, 29, 30, 31, 36, 104, 131, 134: supplied by Anonymous UFS

pp. 92: supplied by Anonymous Univen

pp. 167: supplied by Antonio Erasmus

pp. 140, 141: supplied by Anyway Mikioni

pp. 54, 94, 144: supplied by Asandiswa Bomvana

pp. 56, 68: supplied by Azania Simthandile Tyhali

pp. 38: supplied by Blessing Mavhuru

pp. 71, 72, 79, 112: supplied by Bob Sandile Masango

pp. 48, 127, 185: supplied by Dimakatso Ngobeni

pp. 93, 98, 124: supplied by Frans Sello Mkwele

pp. 70, 79: supplied by Hlulani C. Chabalala

pp. 26, 126, 130: supplied by Kamohelo Maphike

pp. 178: supplied by Keamogetse G. Morwe

pp. 34, 60, 135, 183: supplied by Kulani Mlambo

pp. 74: supplied by Lesley Ngazire

pp. 51, 78, 124: supplied by Litha Dyomfana

pp. 132: supplied by Madoda Ludidi

pp. 50: supplied by Ncedisa Bemnyama

pp. 7, 52, 191: supplied by NRF project team

pp. 184: supplied by Seipati Mokhema

pp. 69, 125, 144: supplied by Siphelele Mancobeni

pp. 40, 66, 128, 133: supplied by Siphephelo Mthembu

pp. 91: supplied by Siyasanga Ndwayi

pp. 45, 65, 80, 172: supplied by Sphelele Khumalo

pp. 170: supplied by Tania Fraser

pp. 96, 100, 136: supplied by Thabo Mpho Miya

pp. 127, 132, 171: supplied by Thalente Hadebe

pp. 175: supplied by Thierry M. Luescher

pp. 33, 100, 181: supplied by Tshepang Mahlatsi

pp. 31, 138, 145: supplied by Tshepo Raseala

pp. 174: supplied by Tshireletso Letsoalo

pp. 51, 101, 148: supplied by Xola Zatu

pp. 110, 146: supplied by Yolokazi Mfuto

REFERENCES

Ahmed, A.K. (2019). *The rise of fallism: #RhodesMustFall and the movement to decolonize the university.* [Doctoral thesis, Columbia University]. ProQuest Dissertation and Theses Global. https://www.proquest.com/docview/2187693841?pq-origsite=gscholar&fromopenview=true

Altbach, P.G. (1991). *Student political activism.* In I*nternational higher education: An encyclopedia.* Garland.

Althusser, L. (1971). Ideology and ideological state apparatuses. In *Lenin and philosophy and other essays.* Monthly Review Press.

Amholt, T.T., Dammeyer, J., Carter, R. & Niclasen, J. (2020). Psychological well-being and academic achievement among school-aged children: A systematic review. *Child Indicators Research*, 13, 1523–1548. https://doi.org/10.1007/s12187-020-09725-9

Badat, S. (1999). *Black student politics, higher education & apartheid: From SASO to SANSCO, 1968–1990.* HSRC.

Biko, S. (1979). *I write what I like.* Heinemann.

Booysen, S. (Ed.). (2016). *Fees Must Fall: Student revolt, decolonisation and governance in South Africa.* Wits University Press.

Bourdieu, P. (1991). *Language and symbolic Power.* Polity Press.

Bücker, S., Nuraydin, S., Simonsmeier, B.A., Schneider, M. & Luhmann, M. (2018). Subjective wellbeing and academic achievement: A meta-analysis. *Journal of Research in Personality*, 74, 83–94. https://doi.org/10.1016/j.jrp.2018.02.007

Cele, M.B.G. (2015). *Student politics and the funding of higher education in South Africa: The case of the University of the Western Cape, 1995–2005.* [Unpublished doctoral thesis, University of the Western Cape].

Cele, M.B.G., Luescher, T.M. & Barnes, T. (2016). Student actions against paradoxical post-apartheid higher education policy in South Africa: The case of the University of the Western Cape. In T.M. Luescher, M. Klemenčič & J.O. Jowi, *Student politics in Africa: Representation and activism* (pp. 182–201). African Minds.

Chávez, M. & Ramrakhiani, S. (2020). Resist: An exploration of student activists' partnerships with faculty and Student Affairs. *Journal of Student Affairs, Research and Practice*, 58(5), 9–12. https://doi.org/10.1080/19496591.2020.1784748

Chikane, R. (2018). *Breaking a rainbow, building a nation: The politics behind #MustFall movements.* Picador Africa.

Clarke, V. & Braun, V. (2014). *Thematic analysis.* In *Encyclopaedia of Critical Psychology* (pp. 1947–1952). Springer.

Collins, P.H. (2019). *Intersectionality as critical social theory.* Duke University Press.

Cooperrider, D.L. & Whitney, D. (1999). *Appreciative inquiry*. Berrett-Koehler.

Cornell, J., Ratele, K. & Kessi, S. (2016). Race, gender and sexuality in student experiences of violence and resistances on a university campus. *Perspectives in Education*, 34(2), 97–119. https://doi.org/10.18820/2519593X/pie.v34i2.8

Curry-Stevens, A. (2011). Persuasion: Infusing advocacy practice with insights from anti-oppression practice. *Journal of Social Work*, 12(4), 1–9. https://doi.org/10.1177/1468017310387252

Daiute, C. & Fine, M. (2003). Youth perspectives on violence and injustice. *Journal of Social Issues*, 59(11), 1–14. 10.1111/1540-4560.00001

Dalton, J.C. & Crosby, P. (2007). Troubled students on campus: Private lives and public responsibilities. *Journal of College and Character*, 8:4. https://doi.org/10.2202/1940-1639.1608

Degenaar, J. (1990). The concept of violence. In N.C. Manganyi & A. du Toit, *Political violence and the struggle in South Africa* (pp. 70-86). Palgrave Macmillan.

Della Porta, D. & Diani, M. (2006). *Social movements: An introduction* (2nd edition). Blackwell Publishing.

Department of Education. (1997). *Education white paper 3: A programme for the transformation of higher education*. Government Gazette No. 18207.

Department of Higher Education and Training. (2013). *White paper for post-school education and training: Building an expanded, effective and integrated post-school system*. DHET.

Fanon, F. (1990 [1961]). *The wretched of the Earth*. Penguin Books.

Farmer, P. (1996). On suffering and structural violence: a view from below. *Daedalus*, 125(1), 261-283.

Freire, P. (2000). *Pedagogy of the oppressed*. Continuum.

Galtung, J. (1990) Cultural violence. *Journal of Peace Research* 27(3), 291-305.

Grosfoguel, R. (2007). The epistemic decolonial turn: Beyond political-economy paradigms. *Cultural Studies*, 21(2-3), 211-223.

Habib, A. (2019). *Rebels and rage: Reflecting on #FeesMustFall*. Jonathan Ball Publishers.

Haraway, D. (1988). Situated knowledges: the science question in feminism and the privilege of partial perspective. *Feminist Studies*, 14(3), 575-599.

Heleta, S. (2016). Decolonisation of higher education: Dismantling epistemic violence and Eurocentrism in South Africa. *Transformation in Higher Education*, 1(1). http://dx.doi.org/10.4102/the.v1i1.9

Hobsbawm, E.J. (1973). *Revolutionaries: contemporary essays.* Weidenfeld and Nicolson.

Hobsbawm, E. (1998). *Uncommon people: Resistance, rebellion and jazz.* Weidenfeld & Nicolson.

Hoefer, R. (2006). *Advocacy practice for social justice.* Lyceum.

Isaacs, S.A. & Savahl, S. (2014). A qualitative inquiry investigating adolescents' sense of hope within a context of violence in a disadvantaged community in Cape Town. *Journal of Youth Studies,* 17(2):269–278. doi:10.1080/13676261.2013.815703

Isaacman, A. (2003). Legacies of engagement: scholarship informed by political commitment. *African Studies Review,* 46(1), 1-41.

Ivtzan, I., Lomas, T., Hefferon, K. & Worth, P. (Eds). (2015). *Second wave positive psychology: Embracing the dark side of life.* Routledge.

Jacobs, S. (2015). The youths. *Africa is a Country* (blog), 04 September 2017. https://africasacountry.com/2017/09/the-youths.

Jansen, J. (2017). *As by fire: The end of the South African university.* Tafelberg.

Jansen, J. (Ed.). (2019). *Decolonisation in universities: The politics of knowledge.* Wits University Press.

Kelly, R.D.G. (2016). Black study, black struggle. *Boston Review: A political and literary forum.* http://bostonreview.net/forum/robin-d-g-kelley-black-study-black-struggle accessed on 22 October 2020.

Kessi, S. & Cornell, J. (2015). Coming to UCT: Black students, transformation and discourses of race. *Journal of Student Affairs in Africa,* 3(2), 1–16. https://doi.org/10.14426/jsaa.v3i2.132

Khanyile, B. (2021). Violences in the South African student movement. In S. Swartz, A. Cooper, C.M. Batan & L. Kropff Causa, The *Oxford handbook of Global South youth studies* (pp. 185–200). Oxford University Press. https://doi.org/10.1093/oxfordhb/9780190930028.013.16

Langa, M. (Ed.). (2017). *#Hashtag: Analysis of the #FeesMustFall movement at South African universities.* CSVR.

Lomas, T. & Ivtzan, I. (2016). Second wave positive psychology: Exploring the positive-negative dialectics of wellbeing. *Journal of Happiness Studies,* 17, 1753–1768. https://doi.org/10.1007/s10902-015-9668-y

Luescher, T.M. (2018). Altbach's theory of student activism in the twentieth century: Ten propositions that matter. In J. Burkett, *Students in twentieth century Britain and Ireland.* Palgrave Macmillan.

Luescher, T.M., Klemenčič, M. & Jowi, O.J. (Eds). (2016). *Student politics in Africa: Representation and activism.* African Minds.

Luescher, T.M., Webbstock, D. & Bhengu, N. (Eds). (2020). *Reflections of South African student leaders, 1994 to 2017.* African Minds.

Luescher, T.M., Wilson Fadiji, A., Morwe, K. & Letsoalo, T.S. (2021). Rapid Photovoice as a close-up, emancipatory methodology in student experience research: The case of the student movement violence and wellbeing study. *International Journal of Qualitative Methods*, 20:1–6. https://doi.org/10.1177/16094069211004124

Mandyoli, L. (2019). *State and civil society: #FeesMustFall movement as a counter-hegemonic force? A case of the University of the Western Cape experience.* [Master's thesis, University of the Western Cape]. University of the Western Cape Research Repository. https://etd.uwc.ac.za/xmlui/bitstream/handle/11394/6567/mandyoli_m_ems_2019.pdf

Madonsela, T. (2021). 3rd annual Social Justice Summit interview. SAfm Sunrise [Radio Broadcast]. Safm. 7 October 2021. https://omny.fm/shows/safm-sunrise-1/playlists

Makhubu, N. (2020). On apartheid ruins: Art, protest and the South African social landscape. *Third Text*, 34(4-5), 569-590. https://doi.org/10.1080/09528822.2020.1835331

Martela, F. & Steger, M.F. (2016). The three meanings of meaning in life: Distinguishing coherence, purpose, and significance. *The Journal of Positive Psychology*, 11(5), 531–545. https://doi.org/10.1080/17439760.2015.1137623

Mbembe, A.J. (2016). Decolonizing the university: New directions. *Arts and Humanities in Higher Education*, 15(1), 29 – 45.

Mignolo, W. (2011). *The darker side of western modernity: Global futures, decolonial options.* Duke University Press.

Morwe, K.G. (2021). *Culture of violence as a mechanism to solve problems with authority among students at South African universities.* [Doctoral thesis, University of Malaga and University of the Free State]. Institutional Repository University of Málaga. https://hdl.handle.net/10630/22878

Morwe, K.G., Luescher, T.M. & Wilson Fadiji, A. (2022). *Restoring wellbeing after student protests: Lessons from #FeesMustFall and its aftermath. A manual for Student Affairs and Services professionals and student leaders.* HSRC.

Naidoo, L. (2020). *Black student intellectuals and the complexity of entailment in the #RhodesMustFall Movement.* [Doctoral thesis, University of the Witwatersrand]. The University of Witwatersrand Research Commons. https://hdl.handle.net/10539/30570

Naidu, E. (2021, March 14). Outrage over death of "innocent bystander" at student protest. *Sunday Independent.* https://www.iol.co.za/sundayindependent/news/outrage-over-death-of-innocent-bystander-at-student-protest-a2551840-46b5-4d2a-85ec-1cd90468ef9d

Ngcaweni, W. & Ngcaweni, B. (Eds). (2018). *We are no longer at ease: The struggle for #FeesMustFall.* Jacana.

Ngidi, N.D., Mtshixa, C., Diga, K., Mbarathi, N. & May, J.D. (2016). "Asijiki" and the capacity to aspire through social media: The #FeesMustFall movement as an anti-poverty activism in South Africa. ICTD '16: Proceedings of the Eighth

International Conference on Information and Communication Technologies and Development, June 2016: 1–11. https://doi.org/10.1145/2909609.2909654

Nkomo, M. (1984). *Student culture and activism in Black South African universities: The roots of resistance.* Greenwood Press.

Ntuli, M.E. (2020). *Implications of student activism on university governance: A multi-case study in South Africa.* [Doctoral thesis, University of KwaZulu-Natal]. https://researchspace.ukzn.ac.za/handle/10413/18914.

Nyamnjoh, F.B. (2016). *#RhodesMustFall: Nibbling at resilient colonialism in South Africa.* Langaa.

Patel, L. (2005). *Social welfare and social development in South Africa.* Oxford University Press.

Raats, C., Adams, S., Savahl, S. & Isaacs, S.A. (2019). The relationship between hope and life satisfaction among children in low and middle socio-economic communities in Cape Town, South Africa. *Child Indicators Research,* 12(2):1–14.

Ryff, C.D. & Singer, B.H. (2008). Know thyself and become what you are: A eudaimonic approach to psychological well-being. *Journal of Happiness Studies,* 9(1), 13–39. https://doi.org/10.1007/s10902-006-9019-0

Sankara, T. (2007 [1987]). The revolution cannot triumph without the emancipation of women. *Speech given on International Women's Day, 08 March 1987.* Thomas Sankara speaks: The Burkina Faso revolution 1983–87. Pathfinder Press.

Schreiber, B. (2018). Mental health at universities: Universities are not in Loco Parentis – students are active partners in mental health. *Journal of Student Affairs in Africa,* 6(2), 121–127. https://doi.org/10.24085/jsaa.v6i2.3318

Soudien, C. (2021). The remaking of South African higher education: A 25-year journey. In W. Pearson & V. Reddy, *Social justice and education in the 21st century: Research from South Africa and the United States* (pp. 131–147). Sprinter Nature.

South African Union of Students (SAUS). (2021, March 15). SAUS calls for national shutdown with immediate effect. *SAUS website: News articles.* https://www.saus.org.za/saus-calls-for-national-shutdown-with-immediate-effect/#:~:text=We%20are%20demanding%20free%20quality,level%201%20of%20the%20lockdown

Strydom, F., Kuh, G. & Loots, S. (Eds). (2017). *Engaging students: Using evidence to promote student success.* SunPress. https://doi.org/10.18820/9781928424093

Swartz, S., Mahali, A., Moletsane, R., Arogundade, E., Khalema, N.E., Cooper, A. & Groenewald, C. (2018). *Studying while Black: Race, education and emancipation in South African universities.* HSRC Press.

Tsang, K.K. (2020). Photovoice data analysis: Critical approach, phenomenological approach, and beyond. *Beijing International Review of Education,* 2:136–152. https://brill.com/view/journals/bire/2/1/article-p136_136.xml

Tinto, V. (2014). Tinto's South Africa lectures. *Journal of Student Affairs in Africa,* 2(2):5–28. https://doi.org/10.14426/jsaa.v2i2.66

Tumubweinee, P. & Luescher, T.M. (2019). Inserting space into the transformation of higher education. *Journal of Student Affairs in Africa*, 7(1), 1–13. https://doi.org /10.24085/jsaa.v7i1.3689

Wallerstein, I. (1997). Eurocentrism and its avatars. *New Left Review*, 226, 93-107.

Wissing, M.P., Wilson Fadiji, A., Schutte, L., Chigeza, S., Schutte, W.D. & Temane, Q.M. (2020). Motivations for relationships as sources of meaning: Ghanaian and South African experiences. *Frontiers in Psychology*, 11:2019.

Yu, L., Shek, D.T.L. & Zhu, X. (2018). The influence of personal wellbeing on learning achievement in university students over time: Mediating or moderating effects of internal and external university engagement. *Frontiers in Psychology*, 8:2287. https://doi.org/10.3389/fpsyg.2017.02287

RESEARCH OUTPUTS AND OTHER RESOURCES OF THE PROJECT

Altbach, P.G. & Luescher, T.M. (2020a, February 5). Another wave of student revolts around the world? *Nexos.*

Altbach, P.G. & Luescher, T.M. (2020b). Another student revolution? *International Higher Education*, Spring 2020, 101, 3-4.

Altbach, P.G. & Luescher, T.M. (2019, December 7). Students are the vanguard in the youth revolution of 2019. *University World News.*

Bosch, T., Luescher, T.M. & Makhubu, N. (2020). Twitter and student leadership in South Africa: The case of #FeesMustFall. In D. Taras & R. Davis, *Power shift? Political leadership and social media.* Routledge. https://doi.org/10.4324/9780429466007

Human Sciences Research Council (HSRC). (2022). *Project website: The new student movement in South Africa: From #RhodesMustFall to #FeesMustFall.* http://www.hsrc.ac.za/en/departments/ied/student-movement

Khanyile, B. (2021). Violences in the South African student movement. In S. Swartz, A. Cooper, C.M. Batan & L. Kropff Causa, *The Oxford handbook of Global South youth studies* (pp. 185–200). Oxford University Press. https://doi.org/10.1093/oxfordhb/9780190930028.013.16

Luescher, T.M. (2018). Tweeting #FeesMustFall: The case of #UCTShutdown. *HSRC Review*, 16(4), 9–11.

Luescher, T.M. (2017). From student enragement to student engagement: What is your theory of change? *HSRC Review*, 5(2), 13–15.

Luescher, T.M. (2016). Towards an intellectual engagement with the #StudentMovements in South Africa. *Politikon: South African Journal of Political Studies*, 43(1):145-148. https://doi.org/10.1080/02589346.2016.1155138

Luescher, T.M. (2016). Frantz Fanon and the #MustFall movements in South Africa. *International Higher Education*, 85, 122–124.

Luescher T.M., Makhubu, N., Oppelt, T., Mokhema, S., & Radasi, M.Z. (2021). Tweeting #FeesMustFall: The online life and offline protests of a networked student movement. In L. Cini, D. della Porta & C. Guzmán-Concha, *Student movements in late neoliberalism: Dynamics of contention and their consequences.* Palgrave Macmillan. https://doi.org/10.1007/978-3-030-75754-0_5

Luescher, T.M., Webbstock, D. & Bhengu, N. (Eds). (2020a). *Reflections of South African student leaders, 1994 to 2017.* African Minds.

Luescher, T.M., Webbstock, D. & Bhengu, N. (2020b). Has co-operative governance failed students? A perspective based on students' experiences. *Kagisano, 12: Student governance and engagement for academic success* (pp. 15–45). Council on Higher Education.

Luescher, T.M., Wilson Fadiji, A., Morwe, K. & Letsoalo, T.S. (2021). Rapid Photovoice as a close-up, emancipatory methodology in student experience research: The case of the student movement violence and wellbeing study. *International Journal of Qualitative Methods*, 20, 1–6. https://doi.org/10.1177/16094069211004124

Morwe, K.G., García-España, E. & Luescher, T.M. (2018). Factors that contribute to student protests at a South African university. *The Social Sciences*, 13(4), 916–926.

Morwe, K.G., Luescher, T.M. & Wilson Fadiji, A. (2022). *Restoring wellbeing after student protests: Lessons from #FeesMustFall and its aftermath. A manual for Student Affairs and Services professionals and student leaders.* HSRC.

South African History Online (SAHO). (2022). *Aftermath: Violence and wellbeing in the context of the student movement – online exhibition.* https://www.sahistory.org.za/exibition/aftermath

Tumubweinee, N.P. & Luescher, T.M. (2019a). Inserting space into the transformation of higher education. *Journal of Student Affairs in Africa*, 7(1), 1-13. https://doi.org/10.24085/jsaa.v7i1.3689

Tumubweinee, N.P. & Luescher, T.M. (2019b). Space, language and identity politics in higher education. *Journal of Student Affairs in Africa*, 7(1), v–xi. https://doi.org/10.24085/jsaa.v7i1.3688

Wilson Fadiji, A., Luescher, T. M. & Morwe, K.G. *(forthcoming)*. The dance of the postives and negatives in life: Student wellbeing in the context of #FeesMustFall-related violence. *South African Journal of Higher Education.*

INDEX